SPIRITUAL FITNESS:
DAY BY DAY

Dear Ray + Barbara,

May these words
nourish your souls.

A brother on the path,

Tom 2/93

By the same author

Generation to Generation
Staying Together
New Men — Deeper Hungers

SPIRITUAL FITNESS: DAY BY DAY

by Tom Owen-Towle

Artwork by Millard Sheets
and Tony Sheets

SUNFLOWER INK
Palo Colorado Canyon   Carmel, Calif. 93923

Library of Congress Catalogue Card No. 89-063710
ISBN 0-931104-21-1

DEDICATION

To my Mother
who taught me that
there was holiness in the daily

INTRODUCTION

*"What I do today is important,
because I am exchanging a day of life
for it."*

Hugh Mulligan

For years I have risen at the crack of dawn, put on a sweatsuit and gone aerobic dancing, jogging, or exercising at a local health spa. I am not alone. Millions of "wellness" advocates across America are out, bright and early, revving up their cardiovascular engines for life's speedway.

We may be overlooking the fact that our minds need limbering up every bit as much as our bodies. We need to fortify our psyches daily with ample spiritual iron. We are whole human beings.

This volume targets those who wish to keep spiritually fit without undue effort or piety. It speaks to adults on the move, leading full, productive lives. Regular doses of inspiration will keep such women and men healthy and on track in the new decade of the 1990s.

Samuel Johnson once wrote: "We more frequently require to be reminded than informed." He was right. Hence, this book of 366 simple reminders to stretch our mental powers, firm our moral muscles, and tone our souls.

SPIRITUAL FITNESS: DAY BY DAY includes an intentional blend of fresh thoughts and old saws, both religious and secular, selected from East and West. My goal has been to furnish the reader with a balanced diet.

vii

These daily devotions will both challenge and comfort, amuse and nudge. All are geared to fight flabbiness of conscience and lethargy of mind.

Here are some easy yet effective ways to use these daily soul exercises.

1) Read each meditation, then close with moments of quiet reflection or prayer.

2) Read the devotion through several times during the day, gaining different insights with each reading.

3) Write a commentary in the margin or compose an inspirational message of your own—maybe even a rebuttal!

4) Use these spiritual health tips as a spur to journal writing.

5) Use the ideas contained in SPIRITUAL FITNESS: DAY BY DAY to provide fodder for conversation with family members around the breakfast or dinner table.

6) Close your day by reading these life-affirming sentiments, to help you clear unresolved angers and lingering clutter.

7) Use SPIRITUAL FITNESS: DAY BY DAY for staff or board meetings.

8) Read the same daily message that your partner reads, even though at different times; then plan moments for sharing when your paths rejoin.

Friends or family members living in different parts of the country are bonded knowing they are each reading the same thoughts that day. It creates a spiritual embrace across the miles.

Where should you keep this volume?

On your bedstand or meal table, on your desk at work or in your bathroom alongside other worthy journals—the key is to have it close at hand for easy use.

In a gym workout, a friend recently said to me: "Tom, I have taken care of my body, off and on, for years. My program has never really worked because I am *off* as often as I am *on*. Then I woke up to the fact that this is the only body I have, so I had better take good, constant care of it. I decided, then and there, to exercise some every day for the rest of my life. You could say that I plan to be a LIFER with respect to physical fitness!"

This book of 366 daily reminders for the 1990s invites you to be a LIFER, too, in the crucial pursuit of keeping your spirit hale and hearty, taut yet supple.

JANUARY

A FRESH START

"Don't let yesterday use up too much of today."

Will Rogers

The past has passed.

Thanks be for our yesterdays. After all, it took a multitude of them to arrive at today.

But the past dare not govern what goes on this new year. Broken promises or sentimental reminiscences can contaminate our current lives.

Last year is gone. We are creating a never-before year, utterly fresh, starting right now.

SPIRITUAL MENU

"One ought, every day at least, to hear a little song, read a good poem, see a fine picture and, if possible, speak a few reasonable words."

Goethe

Hear a little song: a soothing, upbeat tune. If you're up to it, sing a snatch. If the ability is yours, write lyrics or compose a melody line, your theme song for days ahead.

Read a good poem: one you haven't shared before. Speak it out loud.

See a fine picture; a painting, cartoon, or movie will do. Or draw something. Draw your insides out.

Speak a few reasonable words; if no one is nearby to hear them, deliver them to yourself.

Launch your New Year by enjoying spiritual delicacies. They may become staples in your diet.

BLESSED ARE THE MEEK

"Blessed are the meek, for they shall inherit the earth."

Matthew 5:5

We link the words "meek" and "little." But true meekness is not weakness. It means gentleness. It has sinew. It is not sad resignation.

The meek are not harsh or covetous. They do not trample in brute force. They are humble in the strength of reverence. Others claim only their rights, but the meek are concerned about their duties. In a world where human life is threatened, genuine meekness becomes our final hope.

With meekness comes an astonishing reward—inheritance of the earth. It comes as gift and legacy. It comes because the meek would never seize it. As Madeleine L'Engle puts it:

"We are very blessed that it is the meek who are to inherit the earth, for they can be trusted with it."

3

4 FEAR

"...fear infects and corrupts what it touches."

Lillian Hellman

Thoreau, Roosevelt, Bacon, so many sages throughout history, have warned us that nothing is to be feared as much as fear itself.

Fear can be a sobering, sensible guide. There are times to be respectful and cautious. As someone said, "A good scare can be worth more than good advice." Nevertheless, most of our anxieties fail to be constructive.

Fear tends to immobilize us. It makes us withdraw or tighten up. It traps us.

The New Testament offers this thought: "There is no fear in love, but perfect love casts out fear." (I John 4:18) Yet we humans will never know perfect love. Fear continues to plague us.

Our only course is to make fear work *for* rather than against us. There exists a fine line between helpful and destructive fears. But there is a line.

Our job is to find and walk it.

NARROWMINDEDNESS

"The minds of some people are like the pupils of their eyes: the more light you expose them to, the narrower they become."

Edward Darling

Our world is filled with fanatics who crystallize systems of belief from personal opinions. They write a book or establish a school, therewith elevating their viewpoint into a truth, often, THE truth.

In America there are some 200 religious denominations. The majority of them claim to contain not merely a piece of but the very rock itself.

Eric Hoffer cautions us: "The weakness of a soul is proportionate to the number of truths that must be kept from it."

Truth prevails in an open atmosphere not behind closed doors or fixed hearts.

YOU MAKE A DIFFERENCE

"The only relationship that gave meaning for the claustrophobic life of George Babbit had been with Paul Riesling. But not once in the tragedy of their lives had one been able to say to the other: You make a difference."

Ellen Goodman

No greater gift can we offer another person than to say, "Thank you for making a difference in my life. Your gifts, not always pleasant to receive, cannot be adequately measured or reciprocated. They have changed my direction."

It isn't enough to say these four words, "you make a difference," to our friends. Some of our adversaries deserve them as well.

OUR INNER LIGHTS

"Let your steps be guided by such light as you have."

St. Paul

Unimaginable sources of light are present in our beings, waiting to be turned on.

Each of us can generate ample juice when we are in the dark, despairing, unenlightened. We don't always have to turn to outside resources first.

"This little light of mine, I'm going to let it shine" runs the spiritual. We may be amazed when we turn on our lights.

HASTEN SLOWLY!

Tibetan saint Milarepa remarked, "Hasten slowly!"

This wise counsel applies whether we are contemplating a job change, facing death, or pursuing a daily routine. We earthlings like to live in zones of certitude. However, for us to mature, to edge toward wholeness, we must become adept at honoring both/ands, paradoxes like "hasten slowly."

A good car driver knows whether to apply gas or brakes, motoring ahead in timely fashion.

Our enjoyment on this planet will be enhanced when we learn how to hasten slowly—at home, work, or play.

WHEN ANGRY

*"When angry, count 10 before you speak;
if very angry, 100."*

Thomas Jefferson

Sometimes when we are angry, we would be wise to share our upset immediately rather than "sit on it."

The challenge is to keep our anger from degenerating into rage or hostility. Anger can be a charitable emotion that chastens or confronts in order to restore community. Hostility is the attempt to demean or destroy. Wisdom lies in distinguishing between the two.

As the Hasidim wrote: "Since I have tamed my anger, I keep it in my pocket. When I need it, I take it out."

YESES COST!

*"Being able to say 'Yes' means a
willingness to pay a price."*

Caesar Chavez

No gets us off the hook, and *Maybe*
places us on the fence. *Yes* costs time,
energy, imagination, and resources.

An existence void of a yes or a
commitment will prove safe and secure
but meaningless. Without risking yes, we
humans experience little joy or sorrow.
We waddle about in the land of blah.
Unfortunately, contemporary society is
surfeited with yes-butters and no-wayers.

I invite us to say yes to that which
matters, yes to the persons who are
precious to us.

It's worth the price!

THANKING THOSE NEAREST

"If the only prayer you say in your whole life is Thank You, that would suffice."

Meister Eckhart

In 1935, e.e. cummings published a book of poetry with funds provided by his mother. The dedication went: "No Thanks to: Farrar and Rinehart, Simon and Schuster, Coward-McCann, Limited Editions, Harcourt, Brace, Random House, Equinox Press, Smith and Haas, Viking Press, Knopf, Dutton, Harper's, Scribner's Covici, and Friede."

All of the above publishers had rejected his manuscript.

To make public his ingratitude, as cummings did here, is not as impressive as his eagerness to thank his mother for her unswerving support.

He described his mother "as the most completely and humanly generous person I ever knew."

We need to thank those nearest and dearest to us during our lifetimes.

AGITATION ISN'T MY JOB

"People have to make up their minds what their job is and stick to that. I know that agitation isn't my job."

Walter Lippmann

Lippmann penned this line to Upton Sinclair in 1914.

It is important, during the course of our lives, to figure out what kind of human being we can best be. We are creatures with distinctive styles and gifts.

Some of us are naturally abrasive and can use our contentiousness to creative, even compassionate, advantage. We are agitators.

Others have a serene temperament or exude gentleness.

We each have a supreme way to declare our inner character.

CLING TO THE WRECKAGE

"When you're in a spot of trouble, if you can swim you try to strike out for the shore. You invariably drown. As I can't swim, I cling to the wreckage and they send a helicopter out for me. That's my tip, if you ever find yourself in trouble, cling to the wreckage!"

John Mortimer

The title of Mortimer's autobiographical ruminations is an apt metaphor for life. Whenever we are in the throes of a catastrophe, be it accidental or self-imposed, emotional or physical, we can do one of several things to escape.

We can try to swim to a shore which lies miles beyond our reach.

We can wait for a ship, an unlikely prospect.

We can cling to whatever wreckage floats in the vicinity. Then, if we're fortunate, a helicopter may spot us.

GROWING IN DEPTH

"I have to grow in a different way, not cover mileage, but in depth."

Anaïs Nin

When our days near their end, we will be asked, or ask ourselves: how deeply did we give, how deeply did we struggle, how deeply did we devote ourselves to the principles and persons we cherish?

The spiritual way is the deep way: depth as gratitude, depth as love, depth as forgiveness, depth as courage, depth as joy, depth as wonder, depth as conviction.

In one of Alan Paton's South African novels, a character said of going to heaven, "When I go up there, which is my intention, the Big Judge will say to us, 'Where are your wounds?' And if I haven't any, God will say, 'Was there nothing to fight for?' I couldn't face that question," concludes Paton's character.

We will be known by the depth of our convictions and commitments. Life is not a smorgasboard so much as a partisan experience.

We are charged to go, give, love deeply.

14

FROM EYES TO HEARTS

"That old law about 'an eye for an eye' leaves everybody blind."

Martin Luther King, Jr.

That old law resembles the distasteful current emphasis on "getting even." A sense of revenge permeates our world. The result: everyone is irreparably wounded in the fray.

Individuals, tribes, and nations need to rise up and say: "Compassion must triumph over retaliation!"

Religion is a matter of mercy over justice. As Sam Levenson wrote: "We may not always see eye to eye, but we can try to see heart to heart."

Martin Luther King, Jr. was born this date in 1929.

ONE LIFE

"One of the most significant facts about us may finally be that we all begin with the natural equipment to live a thousand kinds of life but end in the end having lived only one."

Clifford Geertz

Our lives are conditioned by factors of heredity and environment. There are things we won't be or do because of our origins.

Once we have paid homage to our roots, it is time to forge our futures. We have sufficient flexibility to shape singular lives. As one wit mused, "Destiny may shape our ends, but we are able to shape our middles!"

We have one good, full shot at creating the kind of life we desire on earth.

SMILES GO AND COME

"The smile that you send out returns to you."

Indian proverb

A smile requires fewer muscular movements than a scowl. A smile warms our own insides as well as occasioning happiness in others. Real smiles, not fake ones.

The same holds for gestures of genuine kindness such as embraces. When we hug another person in fondness and appreciation, we not only give out joy, we also bring back joy to ourselves. Giver and receiver are blessed in the process.

A yell begets a yell.

One smile is likely to beget another.

DROP IT!

The story is told about the Buddha, who one day was sought out by an ardent follower who had brought presents to the master to show devotion. The Buddha gave her an audience. The woman stepped forward and held out her right hand, offering a priceless ivory ornament. "Drop it," said Buddha.

The surprised woman obeyed and stepped back. Then she stepped forward again, this time offering in her left hand a precious jewel. "Drop it," said Buddha. Again the disciple, surprised, obeyed and stepped back.

Then, smiling as if catching the Buddha's meaning, she held out both hands empty and stepped forward. "Drop it," said Buddha.

What do we prize most: our talents, possessions, independence, prestige, our...? Sometimes all we have must be laid aside, consciously and voluntarily. Our hands must be empty if we are to receive, empty if we are to give.

A difficult lesson for us Westerners.

WHY?

*"The father sat in the garden and
contemplated the grass and the tree and
the bird in the tree. And the small child
contemplated his father. And the child
asked: 'Why?' and the father smiled and
said: 'I was about to ask you the same
question.' And he wondered: 'Is this child
as old as I am or am I as young as this
child?'"*

William Barnett

There are wisdoms we parents
transmit to our children before they
vacate the nest. There are learnings they
pass on to us as well.

Then there are those prized
moments when we turn to each other
and offer up the same imponderables:
Why is there life on this planet? Who are
we humans anyway? What happens after
death?

We elders have spent more time
wrestling with these questions than our
younger comrades, but none of us
possesses satisfactory answers.

We are all wonderers in the face of
the mysteries and glories of the universe.

Parents and children serve one
another best by exchanging notes.

GAPS AND INTERLUDES

"It's important not to have one's life all blocked out. It is essential to leave gaps and interludes for spontaneous action."

Jean Hersey

I am prone to overfill my agenda. My days show insufficient changes of pace.

I know why. I grew up feeling that "lazy" was a dirty four-letter word rather than a necessary one. Yet even the chimpanzees have been reported sitting absolutely still watching a sunset, as if fascinated by the spectacle. If they can, surely we humans can take quiet time-outs.

It is the gaps that bring us daily nourishment.

Interludes can be our salvation.

SIGNIFICANCE

"As long as there have been humans we have searched for our place in the cosmos. Where are we? Who are we? We find that we live on an insignificant planet of a humdrum star lost in a galaxy tucked away in some forgotten corner of a universe. We make our world significant by the courage of our questions and by the depth of our answers."

Carl Sagan

We humans dread not death but extinction without significance. What matters to us is that we count. As Thoreau said: "It's not enough just to be good; we need to be good for something!"

We make our world significant "by the courage of our questions and by the depth of our answers!"

Some of our questions are flimsy and foolish. Let us bring courage to our querying.

Some of our answers are shallow and trite. Let us risk depth in our responses.

FRIENDS IN BOTH PLACES!

Attending a large dinner party, Mark Twain sat in silence as the guests talked about eternal life and future punishment. Finally, a lady nearby asked, "Why do you not say anything? I would like to hear your opinion."

Twain replied gravely, "Madam, you must excuse me. I am silent of necessity. I have friends in both places!"

The truth is that our buddies are flawed and our foes exhibit certain virtues. Such a mixed review of humanity keeps our attitudes balanced, quivering between excessive criticism and praise.

HANDS IN THE DARK

"We have a long, long way to go. So let us hasten along the road, the road of human tenderness and generosity. Groping, we may find one another's hands in the dark."

Emily Greene Balch

Emily Greene Balch received the Nobel Peace Prize in 1946 for her unceasing efforts on behalf of world peace.

We "have a long, long way to go" before we achieve global justice, before we can sleep in peace. We need to "hasten along" the only road worth traveling, namely, "the road of human tenderness and generosity."

If we are groping, neither despairing nor battling, if at least we are groping, we have a chance to "find one another's hands in the dark" and then join them in bonds of universal solidarity.

A CHIPPED EDGE

"Must we wait until our hands are clean to reach out to help? No. The reason we can help others discover their gifts, is because each of us has a chipped edge. We all have some fault in need of healing."

Dody Donnelly

I severely broke my elbow years ago.

It has hounded me as a source of pain and frustration ever since. Among my learnings has been a deepened awareness of my fragility: the physical, emotional, and intellectual "chipped edges" of my being.

I am not whole.

I am now a more understanding helper and helpee.

THE SECOND LOOK

"I have lived in this world just long enough to look carefully the second time into things that I am the most certain of the first time."

Josh Billings

Mid-lifers and elders have insights to share with the young because of second looks.

We have lived long enough to flub things yet rebound.

We have lived long enough to believe naively, doubt vigorously, then affirm deeply.

We have lived long enough to forgive without forgetting, persevere without trampling, love without clutching.

STRETCH BEFORE BOWING

"There is an ABC ignorance that precedes knowledge and a doctoral ignorance that comes after it."

Montaigne

We have to earn the right to be wrong. We need to push and stretch our minds as far as they can go, then bow to the mysteries.

Newton said that he felt like a young boy playing with pebbles on the seashore. Thomas Aquinas, at the end of his life, declared that his great *Summa* was little more than rubbish. Those two traveled a long ways before such admissions.

Wise people know how meager their knowledge is.

THIS IS A COMMUNITY

*"When the stranger says: 'What is the
meaning of this city? Do you huddle close
together because you love each other?'
What will you answer? 'We all dwell
together to make money from each other'
or 'This is a community'?"*

T.S. Eliot

Tribes, cities, even civilizations
won't last long if they dwell on "making
money from each other." Self-
aggrandizement and exploitation creep in
when economics reign supreme.

In our nuclear age, unless
communities of all shapes and sizes
embody love, our world will self-destruct.

Love may be too idealistic a goal,
but respect, justice, and tolerance among
peoples are not too much to expect from
us humans.

Were we not born through and for
community?

PRIZES

"All anybody needs to know about prizes is that Mozart never won one."

Henry Mitchell

In Wolfgang Amadeus Mozart's thirty-five years of existence, he never garnered a particular prize. There was no evidence of a trophy case in his den.

Mozart won acclaim during his lifetime, more than many musical geniuses in history, but prizes were not central to his creativity.

The gifted and graceful giants of humanity have been driven to greatness by interior vision more than external carrots.

I am not asking us to eschew awards. Certain ones are desirable. I treasure some I have received, but they were never life-motivators.

The quest for excellence and beauty is inspired from within rather than without.

A LOVE LETTER

"When I was a child, my father was so ignorant that I was ashamed to have him go out among people. But when I grew up I was amazed at how much the old man had learned in such a few short years."

Mark Twain

As we age, our perspective matures.

My Dad and I always had areas of visceral kinship. There were holes, too. But our relationship came into its own fifteen years ago when I wrote him a long-overdue love letter.

It described all the specifics of my unswerving devotion to him.

He returned one to me.

We both carried them on our persons until he died.

My Dad was born on January 29, 1906.

I still love you, Dad.

PAYING ATTENTION

"Tell me to what you pay attention and I will tell you who you are."

George Santayana

Attention means giving more than passing thought to something. Attention results in serious intentions or aims and contentions or claims.

To what do you pay heed in your life?

Go back over today or yesterday. Make notes. Are you paying attention to those things that matter to you?

Are you giving focus and weight to the people, institutions, and challenges that feed you?

UPON THY HEART

"'And these words which I command thee
this day, shall be upon thy heart.' The
verse does not say: 'in thy heart'. For there
are times when the heart is shut. But the
words lie upon the heart, and when the
heart opens in holy hours, they sink deep
down into it."

Hasidic saying

We need to share our cherished
convictions all along the way, for we
know not when our children will be ready
to receive them.

I am not talking about harping away
at them. Wisdom cannot be hammered
into another, but it can flow when the
time is ripe and the ground is prepared.

I have seen wisdoms sink deep down
into families.

FEBRUARY

THE HEART OF DEMOCRACY

"Democracy is based upon the conviction that there are extraordinary possibilities in ordinary people."

Harry Emerson Fosdick

Churchill once noted that democracy is the worst form of government except for all the others. It is a flawed process, a vulnerable system, but a good and fair one.

One strength of democracy is its unyielding, even if chastened, optimism. It believes in human nature when evidence might indicate otherwise.

Democracy is relentless in its "conviction that there are extraordinary possibilities in ordinary people."

We earthlings covet a system like that. Sometimes we even deserve it.

REAL JOY

"Real joy is a serious matter."

Seneca

Joy is more than pleasure or happiness.

It enables us to remain uplifted amid unpleasant or unhappy plights.

Joy has sufficient staying power. It endures. There is nothing fleeting about it.

Joyous people are lighthearted not frivolous, serious without being grim.

When our lives come to a close, may our parting be such as described in Isaiah (55:12):

"For you shall go out in joy, and be led forth in peace; the mountains and the hills before you shall break forth into singing, and all the trees of the field shall clap their hands."

MAGIC

"We have scrubbed the world clean of magic."

Alan Watts

Something catches us off guard, leaves our head shaking and mind spinning. It's magical.

One can get lost in magic. One can worship the occult. Magic is harmful if it diminishes our sense of objectivity. The role of magic is to remind us to honor our logical *and* mystical sides.

Magic keeps us from being too ponderous about things. It opens us to surprises. It keeps us playful. It alerts us to portions of life which remain beyond our figuring and control.

Magic reminds us to pay heed to what Evelyn Newman calls "the constant sacrament of the little moments."

THE GREATEST LOSS

"Death is not the greatest loss in life. The greatest loss is what dies inside us while we live."

Norman Cousins

Living deaths are the most excruciating ones.

The will to enrich our partnership slips away. The desire to excel at our work wanes. We "tank the match" as tennis players say. We give up. Our country forgets, even abrogates, the purpose of its founders.

There are countless ways in which something "dies inside us while we live."

PLEASE RAISE YOUR HAND

"Listen! He says, 'I want to tell you about myself.' 'Hurry!' She says. 'I've got a story too.'"

Joseph Lonero

A speaker opened her remarks by saying, "My job is to speak; your job is to listen. If you finish before I do, please raise you hand."

This happens in living room conversation, too. Chatting away with fervor and assumed eloquence, the eyes of our friend betrays the fact that he or she is no longer with us. They are elsewhere.

The trick is to close out our talking while others still hunger for more.

Dialogue is a mutual activity.

A LIFELONG BATTLE

"Do you know, Fontanes, what astonishes me most in this world? The inability of force to create anything. In the long run the sword is always beaten by the spirit."

Napoleon Bonaparte

Military wizards like Napoleon have been enmeshed in the vortex of violence and know whereof they speak.

Napoleon doesn't claim that force is unable to destroy anything. The limit of brute power is its incapacity "to create anything."

For the spirit to defeat the sword, however, will require energy, bravery, and persistence.

We keep our moral sanity by being wagers of peace.

The battle lasts our lifetimes.

THE LITTLE THINGS

"Little things console us because little things afflict us."

Blaise Pascal

The simple gestures, the insignificant deeds, the mundane decisions cannot be underestimated in life. Most of us ignore little things and wait for big ones. But it is invariably the little things that make or break our days.

Cartoonist Jules Ffeiffer talks about the "little murders" which gnaw away at our loves. It is the petty irritations that erode our friendships.

Conversely, it is the little healings that save and serve our lives, moment by moment.

Little things both console and afflict us.

TIMING

"I believe that a sign of maturity is accepting deferred gratification."

Peggy Cahn

A person was complaining to her tailor about the delay in making a new suit. "Six weeks!" she protested. "Why, the world was created in six days."

"I know," countered the tailor, "and just look at it!"

Most would say the universe took not days but aeons to emerge. Additionally, the majority of tailors work more rapidly than this one. But the point holds.

We are accustomed to quick results. We can't stand still for six months, let alone six weeks or six days. Everything has to happen right here, right now. We are a culture enslaved to instant gratification.

Let's hear it for jobs well done and relationships well ripened.

A RARE PATTERN

"I too am a rare pattern, as I wander down the garden paths."

Amy Lowell

Today is the birthday (1874) of Amy Lowell, American poet, literary critic, and Pulitzer Prize winner in 1926.

We humans hold much in common. We are made of flesh and bones, dreams and frailties. Nonetheless, we are each "a rare pattern." Every one of us is irrepeatable and precious.

We are not just chaotic, disjointed beings. We are rare *patterns.* When we observe the movements and strokes of our lives, we notice wondrous patterns, all our own.

TALKING TO OUR RELATIVE

"Speak to the earth and it shall teach thee."

Job 12:8

"Speaking to the earth" means getting to know it intimately. It's not enough to walk the earth or admire it from afar. Climb mountains as well as view them, work in the soil, befriend the elements—such is our human privilege and call.

Let us speak to the earth with the voices of body and soul, then after our say, listen to it, for "it shall teach thee."

Remember the words of the Sioux holy one, Black Elk:

"The earth is sacred and is a relative of ours."

LIFE IS...

"Life is what happens to you when you're making other plans."

Betty Talmadge

Serendipitous things happen, if we are willing to let them. Our plans must be adjustable to allow life to do what it will with us.

We camp for the sake of our children but fall in love with the hobby ourselves. We search for a particular painting but come upon a gorgeous piece of furniture instead. We take an elective course as a filler and end up pursuing the field professionally.

After the death of Rabbi Moshe of Kobryn, one of his disciples was asked, "What was most important for your teacher?" The disciple thought for a moment and replied, "Whatever he happened to be doing at the moment."

AN ASTONISHED HEART

"Delight in your children openly. Look at them with the widest eyes you can manage, and don't be ashamed to be seen at wonder. You will not see their likes again. What a shame if they should leave without ever knowing they have been beheld and offered up by an astonished heart."

Robert Capon

We have numerous gifts to offer and receive from our children. But no greater gift can we share than to behold them with delight, wonder, an astonished heart. To treat each child as an irrepeatable, growing joy.

Beholding them as such puts us in the mood to treat them that way.

There are ample frustrations and deadends in parenting. Through the sad and agonizing moments our affirmations and affections shine forth.

We will never see their likes again.

MIND-STRETCHING

"The mind stretched by a new idea never returns to its original shape."

Ralph Waldo Emerson

There was a woman who heard for the first time about the theory of evolution. It troubled her greatly as she listened to an exposition of its implications. Then she prayed, "God grant that it may not be true, but if it is true, God grant that not many people will hear about it."

Not fearing new ideas is the first step. The second move opens us to fruitful possibilities in a fresh notion. Then there is the willingness to shift our mind-sets, if need be.

Once our minds grow, they can never return to their original shapes.

Re-shaping should be a regular occurrence.

STOPPING TO SWERVE

"If you stop to be kind, you must swerve often from your path."

Mary Webb

To be kind may be a quiet and gentle act, but it demands energy and change. It may be unnoticeable, but always noteworthy.

Our lives normally drive along without sufficient thought for those along the road who might need our love. Mercy means swerving and changing directions.

A life that moves too swiftly for moments of mercy is moving too rapidly.

A Valentine's Day thought.

THE AFTERNOON OF LIFE

"The afternoon of life must also have a significance of its own and cannot be merely a pitiful appendage to life's morning."

Carl Jung

Carl Jung claimed that upon reaching thirty-five years we enter the second half of our lives—the spiritual time when we begin to *inquire* more than *acquire.*

Our afternoon of existence, be it in our forties or sixties or eighties, hankers for service and celebration, giving back to the universe. During the afternoon we can engage in purposeful activities and shed superfluous ones.

It is the season to pursue what Virginia Woolf called "freedom from unreal loyalties." It is the time to reflect, sort out, do what is worthy of our humanity, in the name of the cosmos.

FLUSH AND FILL

The New Testament story goes like this. A man cleans out his home, flushing all available demons. Having done a thorough job, he takes off on a trip. Upon his return, the house is filled with new demons and "the last state becomes worse than the first." (Matthew 12: 43-45)

The problem is that he rid his life of bad habits but failed to put anything good in their place.

It is not sufficient to abolish war, if we have not envisioned peaceful institutions to fill the void. Eliminating the negatives in our lives is crucial but only the initial step. The vacuum must be filled.

We need to denounce *and* announce, eradicate evils *and* create goods.

PLUCK

"Life shrinks or expands in proportion to one's courage."

Anaïs Nin

Every moment of demonstrated bravery en-courages us to meet a similar situation or fresh encounter with fortitude.

There is a pyramiding effect.

Bravery expands us.

We can be bright, well-intentioned, possess a masterful life-plan, but without courage, without pluck, we travel a short distance.

Pluck is that indescribable "oomph" that propels us forward when normal signals urge us to stay put.

Winston Churchill once sent a pudding back to the chef complaining that it "lacked a theme." Moral and spiritual bravery or pluck are themes essential to our world today.

DOING

"I hear and I forget. I see and I remember. I do and I understand."

We may feel love, even hold the attitude of love toward another person, but it has no impact on our sisters and brothers unless we show it.

Henry David Thoreau put it this way: "A truly good book teaches me better than to read it. I must soon lay it down and commence living on its hints...What I began by reading I must finish by acting."

Love lives in action.

They say that children remember 20% of what they hear, 30% of what they see, 50% of what they see and hear, 70% of what they say, and 90% of what they do. I bet the figures run the same for adults.

There is no substitute for hands-on involvement. This goes for emotional and moral work as well as physical labor.

HANDS AND HEART

*"Who shall stand on God's holy mountain?
The one who has clean hands and a pure
heart!"*

Psalm 24

Both hands and heart. Outer
behavior and inner attitude. The
examined, compassionate life requires a
balance between doing and being, action
and reflection. Our hands and hearts, our
whole beings, must be involved in the
good life.

The religious person pursues what
Socrates asked for in the prayer from the
Phaedrus: "May the outward and inward
person be one."

A worthwhile, daily goal.

HANDLE WITH CARE

"We should do things with wood that the wood likes. There are certain things it likes to be used for. When I use wood, I make sure it likes what I'm doing to it."

Buckminster Fuller

Spiritually expansive persons love self and others, nature and God, plants and animals—plus inanimate objects, like wood.

Give thought to how you relate to things surrounding you: your bicycle, hand-made gifts, money, food. Do you handle them with care?

Do unto things as you would have them be with you.

MAKING PEACE WITH LIFE

An adult admonition shared early in my life makes increasing sense: "I have been able, as I age, to make a treaty of peace with life."

This mentor squawked about the inequities of life. She took seriously the struggle to build a better world. She didn't fold up her tent.

The difference was that she stopped taking herself *too* seriously. She no longer ranted and raved about her causes. Her frustrations and bitternesses subsided. She grew more tolerant of herself and others. She quit climbing over walls or people. She became softer and gentler as she matured.

EVEN TO GOD

"I had a presentiment that the true saint was one who resists, struggles, and is not afraid, in time of great need, to say no, even to God."

Nikos Kazantzakis

A full-fledged religious traveler wrestles long and hard with self, others, and divine presence.

But wrestling isn't enough. We also need to "resist." There must be a push and pull in our engagements with ultimate reality. Genuine saints are not weaklings. They have the courage both to surrender and confront, to say yes and no to all that meets them.

They talk back to God.

NIGGARDLINESS

"When you cease to make a contribution, you begin to die."

Eleanor Roosevelt

The story is told of a king who invited his subjects to a banquet. He told each to bring a flask of wine and informed them that the wine would be poured into a large vat.

Each person mused: "What will my small flask of wine mean? I will bring a flask of water and no one will know the difference."

You and I weasle out of sharing our true gifts. We bring water rather than wine. We downplay our talents when the occasion beckons us to reveal them.

For life's celebration to overflow with meaning and nourishment, everyone of us must do our part.

WHAT DOES THE LORD REQUIRE?

"...and what does the Lord require of you but to do justice, and to love kindness, and to walk humbly with your God?"

Micah 6:8

Three invitations.

First, do justice, not just think about or applaud it.

Second, love kindness. Another translation of this Hebrew phrase is "steadfast love." Love is not the primary challenge here. *Steadfast* love is. Love that endures exhilarations, agonies, and blahs.

Third, walk humbly with your God. Not the gods of someone else but *your* God or gods: ones worthy of your service and company.

GOODNESS

*"The good we do for ourselves dies with
us. The good we do for our community
lives forever."*

Anonymous

I would edit this sentiment.

Genuine self-love (not self-
infatuation) is a launching pad for social
compassion. Our activism must issue
from a sense of enlightened self-interest,
otherwise it breeds resentment and
burnout.

We need to do good for ourselves
and others, without getting stuck in
either domain. Religious people are
ambidextrous; they reach within and
without.

I agree with John Dewey who
suggested that we amend the wise
message of the Bible, "sufficient unto the
day is the evil thereof," by its oft-ignored
counterpart, "sufficient unto the day is
the good thereof."

It is difficult to know whether the
good we do will die or live on after us.
That's not ours to determine anyway.

ONE NOTE TO THE NEXT

Somebody asked Pablo Casals, world famous cellist, what was the hardest thing about playing the cello. He replied, "Getting from one note to the next."

This is what absorbs most of our energies, getting by one day at a time, trying to plan intelligently for tomorrow.

George Frazier related a conversation with Duke Ellington. He and Ellington stood out under the stars one night. Frazier looked up at the sky and remarked how beautiful and clear it was, and said: "Duke, it looks like a good day tomorrow."

Ellington retorted: "Friend, any day I wake up is a good day."

We live most passionately and productively when we live from one note to the next.

February 27   SUFFOCATING ON COURTESY

"A person can suffocate on courtesy."

Jerome Lawrence

This is a punch line in Lawrence's play *Inherit the Wind*, the story about the Scopes Trial, the courtroom drama of our century where the freedom of every American was at stake.

I believe in being courteous, gracious, thoughtful. But, like other virtues, you can overdo them. Too much courtesy smacks of saccharine. It becomes faintheartedness.

There are moments when we should assert rather than defer, intervene, push and shove rather than submit.

There are times in our personal interactions when we may be suffocating someone as well as ourselves with gobs of gooey courtesy.

PERSEVERANCE

"Perseverance is not a long race. It is many short races one after another."

Walter Elliot

A marathon is composed of more than four ten-kilometer races. A 10k race us made up of several shorter jaunts.

Good runners break up long races into measurable units. They run certain times for each mile.

Goal setters work in terms of specific, measurable, achievable challenges rather than tackling one gigantic, insurmountable problem.

ONE DAY AT A TIME

"It is only possible to live happily ever after on a day-to-day basis."

Margaret Bonnano

We can plan months in advance. We can lay out a yearly life-plan—even a five-year agenda. Yet we can only tackle our agenda "on a day-to-day basis."

Whether we are pregnant or suffering from terminal illness, on a new job or facing retirement, in or out of a partnership, our happiness is reached by taking one day at a time, hour by hour, minute to minute.

Each moment is precious and to be embraced as such. We are called not to seize time so much as fulfill it.

Welcome Leap Year!

MARCH

PENANCE, CAVORTING, AND WORK

Irish writer Edna O'Brien wanted her life to alternate among penance, cavorting, and work.

Work is a staple in the spiritual life. As my friend remarks, "I love my work and work my love." They are inseparable.

Cavorting is mandatory for the good life. We are healthiest when we romp relaxedly, with no pressing goal in mind.

Penance entails spending time each day forgiving ourselves and others for our failings. It also means doing something to set matters right.

Penance, cavorting, and work, these three in reasonable balance.

March
2   BRING ALONG THINE AX

"If thou wouldst give good advice to the wood chopper, bring along thine ax."

Clinton Lee Scott

Advice to our children, friends, or co-workers is useless without example. Savvy is empty unless backed up by sweat. Our minds and bodies confirm the contributions of our mouths.

In a sermon which Rabbi Mikhal once gave before a large gathering, he said: "My words shall be heeded." And he added immediately: "I do not say: 'You shall heed my words.' I say: 'My words shall be needed. I address myself too. I too must heed my own words!'"

Others will soon forget our eloquence and long remember our ax-work.

MINDS WITH SOUL

*"I went away and cried to the Master of
the Universe, 'What have you done to me?
A mind, like this I need for a son? A heart I
need for a son, a soul I need for a son,
compassion I want from my son, righteous-
ness, mercy, strength to suffer and carry
pain, THAT I want from my son, not a
mind without a soul!'"*

Chaim Potok

This is the poignant reflection of
Rabbi Saunders about his son Daniel in
Potok's novel, *The Chosen*.

I feel the same way about our
children. I want them to use their brain
power to the fullest. I want their minds to
be stimulated and stretched.

However, I hanker for our children
to have hearts that can leap with joy,
endure suffering, and reverberate with
laughter.

I want our children to have minds
with soul.

NEVER TERRIFYING

"Truly great men and women are never terrifying. Their humility puts us at ease."

Elizabeth Goudge

Great people generate respect rather than fright. They don't have overweaning egos. Their power resides in persuasion not control.

Great humans are like salt, which is distinctively itself when it can't be seen and tasted for itself at all, but when it is transforming whatever it is in.

Salt-like people are often in the background. You don't even notice their presence but without them there would be an appreciable loss. They would be sorely missed.

Like salt, great persons make everything they touch more enjoyable—transformed.

March
5   ETHICAL INFANTS

"After several thousand years, we have advanced to the point where we bolt our doors and windows and turn on our burglar alarms—while the jungle natives sleep in open-doored huts."

Morris Mandel

We make scientific advances daily. Even the recalcitrant among us are moving into the computer era.

But while we are nuclear giants, we remain, as General Omar Bradley lamented, "ethical infants."

We break into other people's homes. We cheat in blue-and-white collar ways. We are prejudiced against people of color. We oppress individuals different from ourselves.

We have a long way to go to grow up morally.

One wonders if we will make it to adulthood.

ENJOY THE INTERVAL

"There is no cure for birth and death save to enjoy the interval."

George Santayana

Religion wants us to spend time reflecting upon the puzzles of birth and death. Studying first and last things can prove spiritually beneficial.

However, there is such a thing, as Alan Watts remarked, as *tantum religio*, "too much religion." Religion becomes hazardous to our health when we go beyond probing birth and death and try to "cure" them. Religion gets sidetracked when it seduces us into thinking that our comings and goings can be solved.

The point of existence, after all, is less analysis and more involvement. Our call is to enjoy the interval given us.

THANKFULNESS

*"Now we have finished. Everyone stand
and we will bow to the Buddha three times
to thank him."*

Hsuan Hua

There are three reasons to thank
Buddha.

First, if we did not have a great
enlightenment, we had a small one.

Second, if we did not have a small
enlightenment, at least we did not get
sick.

Third, states the legend, if we got
sick, at least we didn't die.

It is startling how many blessings
come our way in the most uneventful of
days. We can always find things to be
grateful for in our existence.

To stay in spiritual shape we are
encouraged to say "thank you daily."

Gratitude is a way of being alive.

March 8   SIDESWIPED!

"Everytime I think that I'm getting old, and gradually going to the grave, something else happens."

Lillian Carter

Life is filled with delightful detours, if we are looking for them. Some changes of pace happen to us; others we create on our path to the grave.

In either case, the lives of alert, awake, flexible humans display creative change.

As someone noted, "Happiness is the art of making a bouquet of those flowers right around you."

JOY COMES IN THE MORNING

"There may be tears during the night, but joy comes in the morning."

Psalm 30:5

Every night when we retire, my wife, Carolyn, and I try to oust whatever frustrations and angers we might have with ourselves, work, one another, whatever. This ritual cleanses us for sounder sleep.

There remain nights when we are unable to quiet our spirits. Our sleep is punctuated by fears and tears, uneasiness and upset.

We still wait for a new day, high in hope that joy will rise with the sun.

FRIENDS AT MIDNIGHT

One of Jesus' parables tells of the friend at midnight, with its haunting confession of inner bankruptcy: "A friend of mine in her journey has come to me. I have nothing to set before her."

We would like to be hospitable, but we are frenzied. We want to offer guidance to someone, but we are fainthearted. We are wounded healers.

This state of affairs need not be disastrous. When we have no theories or materials to offer, we still have our selves.

Our very presence, without objects, advice, or books, is usually sufficient.

PLANTING FIRMLY

"Be sure that you put your feet in the right place, and then stand firm."

Abraham Lincoln

I am reminded of the humorous yet apt decision of so many folks: "She had her feet planted firmly—in the air."

Location is crucial in life. Finding the right place is half of the challenge in being a professional, a parent, a citizen.

When we make our choices today, let us stand firm without wavering or wobbling.

Until we're back on the move again.

SOME TINY FRAGMENT

"Sometimes I feel that what is inside me is not all of me. There's something else sublime, quite indestructible, some tiny fragment of the universal spirit. Don't you feel it?"

Alexander Solzhenitsyn

I feel part of the greater whole when I experience the majesty of the ocean or camp in the desert amid the stars. My contributions to society also reflect the larger goodness underlying our universe.

What an unspeakable privilege and responsibility to feel connected to the universal spirit.

I resonate with the phrasing of Teilhard de Chardin: "Like the atom, we have no value save for that part of ourselves which passes into the universe."

BORN ORIGINALS

"We are born originals yet we die copies."

Edward Young

Accused by the congregation of altering the service that he inherited from his father, one Hasidic master retorted, "I do exactly as my father did. He did not imitate, and I do not imitate!"

Genuine holy people are not trapped in ego extension. They express religiosity in their own singular ways, and more importantly, invite us to follow suit.

Buddha and Jesus, for example, invited us to be lamps unto ourselves. It was their disciples, who came after them, who promoted conformity.

DEBT TO ENEMIES

"I owe much to my friends, but, all things considered, it strikes me that I owe even more to my enemies."

André Gide

Critics are thorns in our sides. They prick and puncture. They bruise us. Yet, as we heal from the wounds, we grow to appreciate their barbs.

The trouble with friends is they let us get away with too much. Instead of a shove, they may pass us syrup.

Foes have no need to tell us anything but the truth.

**March
15**   **YOUR NAP**

"When you have a lot of things to do, get your nap out of the way first."

Jeremiah Hynes

In busy lives one of the first things to go is rest. Addicted to pressure, we forfeit renewal.

When I am burdened with crises, I take moments out of my datebook for re-creating my spirit. I may not garner a full nap, but a short walk, some meditation, any restful shift will help.

Naps aren't only for little ones. We mid-lifers covet them, too.

SCARS

"A voice said look me in the stars and tell me truly, people of earth...if all the soul-and-body scars were not much to pay for birth."

Robert Frost

Take a close look at your "soul-and-body scars." Center upon one loss, hurt, tragedy. Was it caused from within or without, or both? How did you handle it? What kind of resources were helpful to you? Have you moved through to the other side? If not, what concerns remain?

If you wish, visit some more with the scar. Then, when ready, say farewell to it.

I WILL NOT ALLOW!

"I will not allow one prejudiced person or one million or one hundred million to blight my life. My inner life is mine, and I shall defend and maintain its integrity against all the powers of hell!"

James Weldon Johnson

This personal vow was made during the 1930's by a great black leader. It is the kind of pledge courageous pioneers make when besieged with oppression.

We have to combat external forces simultaneously with shoring up our internal spirits in this struggle called life.

If we compromise our character, we're sunk.

THE BIGGEST ROOM

*"There's always room for improvement.
It's the biggest room in the house."*

Louise Heath Leber

Particular rooms within my favorite homes have brought me delight and solace.

I sought aloneness, and a room furnished it. I wished to express my creative impulses, and I made a room over in my own image.

Wander leisurely about your residence and discover anew those things which comfort or disturb you about the current spaces in which you live. As appropriate, be willing to change your quarters to meet your present aspirations.

There are physical and emotional rooms inside our homes and our beings. The challenge, while we are alive, is to provide both with treasures that are beautiful, enduring, and ours.

A DEADLY SIN

"I matter. You matter. What goes on between us matters."

Virginia Satir

In the Middle Ages the religious leaders listed seven deadly sins which they thought to be the most interesting and original of our human blunders. Their list holds up well for us moderns; pride, covetousness, gluttony, lust, anger, envy, and sloth remain roadblocks to spiritual growth.

Sloth is a deadly sin because it renders us asleep, listless, moribund. At least in the other sins we are kicking, bouncing, struggling. In slothfulness we are stuck as slow, upside-down, limb-hanging, fungus-covered entities.

Sloth mires us in dejection and faintheartedness. We are paralyzed by the belief that we are insignificant. To be slothful is to be indifferent which, in turn, means that we feel that no one, including ourselves, can make a difference on this globe.

We should acknowledge our boundaries and brokenness. We should also proclaim: "I matter. You matter. What goes on between us matters."

TURBULENT JOY

George Bernard Shaw called Beethoven "the most turbulent spirit that ever found expression in pure sound. The power of the Ninth Symphony is the turbulent joy of humanity."

When turbulence runs our lives, everything becomes chaotic, crazy. But that isn't the fault of turbulence. We humans are to blame.

The knack in life is to keep enough turbulence to be expansive without being inundated by it. As Nietzsche wisely commented, "We must have enough chaos in our lives to give birth to dancing stars."

PLANT A TREE

"Those who plant trees love others beside themselves."

English proverb

An elderly Chinese woman, when asked what she would do if this were her final day on earth, said, "I must plant a tree!"

We don't know when we shall die, so it is crucial to plant something daily. We plant trees to provide shade, beauty, growth for those near us and those coming soon. All kinds of trees.

Spring is here.

PRAY FOR STRENGTH

"Do not pray for tasks equal to your powers. Pray for powers equal to your tasks. Then you will wonder at yourself, at the richness of life that comes to you."

Phillips Brooks

We imagine the thrill of an easy life, yet once we arrive at comfort, we guard against boredom.

We creatures yearn to grow. We need challenges, even upsets. We vegetate without them.

Our prayer should not be to have our life free of temptations, but to possess the courage to face them.

A THOUGHT WHOLE

"We must have the courage to think a thought whole."

Soren Kierkegaard

The cowardly among us specialize in partial truths. We stress freedom without talking about its modifier, "responsible." We act as if reason is a pure process without taking into account its correlates: intuition, the unconscious, faith.

Serious and sensible ones in the human family deal with a value from various angles. They juggle the multiple pieces of a thought before making bold claims.

We may never think a thought whole, but we march toward that goal.

RESPECTABLE EVILS

"Slavery disturbs my peace."

Henry David Thoreau

All the respectable evils of mid-19th century America—poverty, war, and slavery—disturbed this morally sensitive laborer for justice.

There should be some economic wrong, social injustice, or moral anguish keeping us restless today. Spiritually awakened people are also peace-disturbers themselves.

What is the issue that throws your soul out of kilter?

How do you plan to address it and restore your equilibrium?

CHANGE ONLY WHEN NECESSARY

Falkland, a martyr of the English Civil War, as he stood facing Hampden and Pym, said: "Mr. Speaker, when it is not necessary to change, it is necessary not to change." Or as the folk wisdom runs: if something works, don't fix it!

Perpetual meddlers have a tendency to tinker with this relationship or that machine. We can't leave well enough alone. We are hell-bent on perfection—unsatisfied with how we look, where we work, and what we achieve.

Sometimes, it is crucial to stay unchanged.

BEING REMEMBERED

*"We must care to know during our
lifetimes how we want to be remembered
in death. This will mold our lives."*

Robert Muller

Muller wanted to be remembered as
one "convincing everybody I could that
to be alive on this planet is a miracle."

Martin Luther King, Jr.'s aspiration
was to be "someone who tried to love
and serve humanity."

Others summarize the purpose of
their lives variously: "carrier of joy,"
"bridge-builder," "plodder to the end,"
"one who lived life to the full," and
"champion of liberty."

We exude different qualities. Each of
us will be remembered in one primary
way.

STILL GOOD TO BE ALIVE

*"And Job said, 'Naked I came from my
mother's womb, and naked shall I return;
the Lord gave and the Lord has taken
away; blessed be the name of the Lord.'"*

Job 1:21

This is one of those infuriating
biblical non-sequiturs. The final
affirmation simply doesn't follow from the
initial claims.

Yet this seeming contradiction lies at
the heart of the spiritual pilgrimage. For
life is good *and* bad. Life graces *and*
undercuts us; nevertheless, we are glad
to be alive.

Often when we receive, we are
willing to praise, and when we are
rejected or injured, we are eager to
condemn. There are moments to applaud
and jeer, but our bedrock feeling must
remain one of thanksgiving.

When I am happy or sad, clear or
befuddled, may I still bless... bless self,
bless neighbor, bless nature, bless
God...ever bless!

ON THE DARKEST NIGHTS

"Why fear the dark? How can we help but love it when it is the darkness that brings the stars to us? What's more, who does not know that on the darkest nights is when the stars acquire their greatest splendor?"

Dom Helder Camara

Tragic moments give perspective to our joyous ones. If we knew no suffering, our happiness would be vacuous.

Most of my dark moments are indispensable to my existence. I would trade few of them away.

How about you?

As the poet May Sarton wrote:

"Help us to be the always hopeful gardeners of the spirit, who know that without darkness, nothing comes to birth. . .as without light, nothing flowers."

**March
29**   **PUT THEM ASIDE**

"Learn your theories well, but put them aside when you touch the miracle of the living soul. Not your theories but your own creative individuality must decide."

Carl Jung

This counsel pertains to our intimate relationships and parenting endeavors as well as our vocational lives.

First of all, we go through the rigors of intellectual pursuit. We study, long and hard, the theories that are relevant to our field. Many contemporaries fail right here—be they artists, engineers or clergy. They want to bypass book learning and jump right into practice.

It is also unfortunate for people to be academically prepared but unable to "cut the mustard" in the field.

Theories are a means toward an end. Wise ones know when to place knowledge in the background.

CREATE *AND* PROTEST

"The hottest places in hell are reserved for those who, in a moment of moral crisis, seek to maintain their neutrality."

Dante

Albert Schweitzer once chided Pablo Casals, the outspoken social idealist, for his controversial public utterances. Schweitzer told Casals that it was better to create than to protest. "No," replied Casals, "there are times when the only creative thing we can do is to protest; we must refuse to accept what is evil or wicked."

Creating and protesting are essential in today's world. We don't have the luxury of choosing only one or the other.

It is not sufficient for the disenchanted to engage in ceaseless protest. They need to spend time producing worthwhile realities too.

Conversely, some people become ivory-tower creators, generating good and beautiful things, but disappearing when the call goes out to resist evil.

Creativity and protest are like our two hands. We use them both.

SELF-GOVERNANCE

"One can decide a lot of things, but personal choices are hard. I tend to wait until one alternative is no longer available, and then inform myself that I have chosen."

Meg Greenfield

Sometimes we are spiritually hamstrung and unable to take charge. On the whole, we do well to make our own decisions rather than have them made for us by others or by circumstances beyond our control.

As a colleague quipped: "People can be divided into three groups: those who make things happen, those who watch things happen, and those who wonder what happened."

We are not in total charge of our lives, but we possess more self-governance than imagined or used.

Being proactive rather than inactive or reactive is a wise life stance.

APRIL

SUFFICIENT SILLINESS

"Everyone is a damn fool for at least five minutes every day; wisdom consists in not exceeding the limit."

Elbert Hubbard

Some of us have trouble being silly and foolish, let alone being that way five minutes every day. The world furnishes us with heavy news which we take too seriously. *Too* is the problem.

Life is a solemn matter but not a grim one. Our days cry out for laughter and lightheartedness, doing zany things. At least five minutes' worth every day.

On April Fool's Day kick off an era of sufficient silliness. Tell a joke, play a prank, laugh heartily every day of April.

Then keep your habit alive.

RELIGIOUS LIBERTY

"I have sworn upon the altar of God eternal hostility against every form of tyranny over the human mind."

Thomas Jefferson

Jefferson was born today in 1743. He was a versatile person who could farm and play the violin, conduct scientific experiments and preside over our country.

He was also of strong religious persuasion. The work of which Jefferson was most proud, as his epitaph indicates, was his labor on behalf of religious liberty in America.

In 1777 he produced his famous Statute for Religious Liberty. It stated that all people should be free to confess their own convictions in matters of religion.

A sound idea for our modern era of religious bigotry and persecution.

A CROSS TO BEAR

Once in handling a divorce case in which the husband enumerated instances of marital suffering, Abraham Lincoln interrupted him and said, "My friend, I regret to hear this; but let me ask you in all candor, can't you endure for a few moments what I have had as my daily portion for the last fifteen years." He spoke so mournfully and with such a look of distress that the husband was completely disarmed.

Abraham Lincoln defected the first time at the planned wedding with Mary Todd. He eventually married her, but he never loved her and she never loved him. This was a sorrowful situation in the life of an otherwise happy and productive person.

As is often the case, we don't know the singular anguish suffered by public figures or even personal friends. It makes us realize that we need to be tender and understanding toward one another.

We all have our particular crosses to bear.

THE ULTIMATE MEASURE

"The ultimate measure of a person is not where they stand in moments of comfort and convenience, but where they stand at times of challenge and controversy."

Martin Luther King, Jr.

Martin Luther King, Jr., a major 20th century black leader in the struggle for racial justice, was killed this date in 1968. He practiced what he preached.

He chose challenge and controversy over comfort and convenience. He believed with Tennessee Williams that a "person without conflict is like a sword cutting daisies."

King did not generate conflict for the sake of personal exploitation. Rather he was willing to risk his position, prestige, and life for equality of all peoples.

King was a great man. More importantly, a good one.

PRINCIPLE OR TASTE?

*"In matters of principle, stand like a rock.
In matters of taste, swim with the current."*

Thomas Jefferson

This is sound counsel for us
befuddled parents trying to do "right" by
our children.

We treat parenting interactions as
equally crucial. We mix up principles and
tastes in nurturing our offspring.

We need to make distinctions in our
parenting. I have learned to stand firm on
issues of trust, honesty, and excellence in
school or work. I try to be flexible with
respect to their choices of music or
extracurricular activities.

I offer my own principles and display
my own tastes to let them know who I
am and what I prefer. Then I back off,
and let them move ahead.

April
6　WASH YOUR BOWL

"I have just entered the fellowship and am anxious to learn the first principle of Zen. Will you please teach it to me?
Chao-Chou responded, 'Have you eaten your supper?'
The novice replied, 'I have.'
'Then go wash your bowl!'"

According to Zen, our quest for ultimate reality is so difficult because we look in obscure places for what lies in broad daylight.

We think religion is esoteric, hidden, strange.

The spiritual journey invites us to pay close attention to the ordinary, the daily, what lies right in front of us.

MAKE THE OBSERVATION YOURSELF

"Aristotle could have avoided the mistake of thinking that women have fewer teeth than men, by the simple device of asking Mrs. Aristotle to keep her mouth open while he counted."

Bertrand Russell

Others have soared and stumbled before us. We learn from our predecessors.

But there are times to experience a delight or solve a problem directly rather than obliquely, through guesswork, or second-hand.

It is our responsibility to show up in person, to make observations ourselves.

HATRED CEASES BY LOVE

"Let us overcome anger by kindness, evil by good. Victory breeds hatred, for the conquered are unhappy. Never in the world does hatred cease by hatred; it ceases by love."

Buddha

Buddha, the great religious prophet, was born in Nepal in 563 B.C. In Japan his birthday is celebrated on April 8th and is called *Hana Matsuri*, the flower festival.

Not all hatred ceases when we show compassion. Yet the hatred within our hearts is stymied when we love. Furthermore, things bloom and flower because of the gentle care and nourishment of love.

May this be a day when we bring something to flowering freshness.

BE OBSCURE CLEARLY

"I know you believe you understand what you think I said, but I'm not sure you realize that what you heard is not what I meant ."

Anonymous

It is a miracle that we humans communicate at all, given our different backgrounds, moods, feelings.

The challenge is to make our messages clear, concise, and compassionate. We begin by being lucid. As E. B. White remarked, "Be obscure clearly!"

The essence of communication is not the subject spoken but the person expressing. If *we* come across, then we have been successful.

Our goal is communion.

ANIMAL LIB

"Heaven goes by favor. If it went by merit, you would stay out and your dog would go in."

Mark Twain

April 10, 1866, the American Society for the Prevention of Cruelty to Animals was chartered in New York State.

We pay homage to our animal companions today—the birds, dogs, and cats who are some of the best friends in our homes or on our block. Of course, we are all animals. As James Thurber put it: "I have always thought of a dog lover as a dog that was in love with another dog."

I remember our beautiful black labrador, Spring. She was hardly faultless. She made messes around the house. She bumped over waste baskets when we "left" her. She exhibited a batch of neuroses. But, oh what faithfulness, what loyalty, what hunger for physical closeness!

May our animal kin enjoy certain inalienable rights: the right to freedom from fear, pain, and suffering, whether in the name of science or sport, fashion or food, exhibition or service.

We must speak for those who can't.

A IS FOR APRIL

"Everything begins with A."

Gertrude Stein

Abraham was a courageous, faithful guide in leading his people into the unknown.

Alive is the way I want to be while breathing.

Aknaton was an Egyptian religious teacher in 1338 B.C. and, according to records, the first leader to proclaim monotheism.

Awake and vigilant must we always be said Buddha, the "awakened one."

Asoka, the king of ancient India, was a rare ruler who majored not in war but peace.

Awful is the universe in its blend of beauty and terror.

Have fun today by listing principles and presences in your story which begin with the letter A.

INDOMITABLE

"Faith is rooted in the will to live. It is like crabgrass. It will not give up. Stone walls are no match for it. It can break through cement. It defies poison and surgery. It is indomitable."

John Wolf

We like to view ourselves as beautiful plants or flowering trees. But the most successful among our species resemble dandelions, weeds, crabgrass. They persevere. They sprout up when least expected and against all odds.

They keep coming back.

In Ernest Hemingway's classic novel of struggle, THE OLD MAN AND THE SEA, there is the description: "Everything about him was old except his eyes and they were the same color as the sea and were cheerful and undefeated."

I invite us to be like crabgrass, like the old man, like the sea: "cheerful and undefeated."

AN HOUR A DAY...

*"A person who doesn't have one hour free
each day is not a human being."*

Martin Buber

Sleep doesn't count. A blank hour
before the next appointment isn't what
Buber had in mind either.

During our days there must be open
times when we choose re-creative
endeavors. Sports, meditation, walks,
non-productive reading qualify.

Albert Schweitzer once said: "Why
could I accomplish so much in life?
Because I gave up sports!" This sacrifice
may have worked for many throughout
history, including one so compassionate
as Schweitzer. He gave up sports
because he was singleminded in his
service to humanity.

The opposite works for me. I need
sports to renew and strengthen me for
the challenges of my agenda. I need
running and tennis to re-create my spirit.
I give up a number of things in order to
keep spiritually focused and fit, but not
sports.

My friend says there is business and
monkey-business. We need at least an
hour of the latter each day.

WE ARE LIKE DWARVES

"We are like dwarves seated on the shoulders of giants; we see more than the ancients, and things more distant—but this is due not to our own stature."

Bernard de Chartres

Our lives are centered upon the here and now, living fully, walking proudly, and contributing compassionately to the life which loved us into being.

We also need perspective. We give thanks to the pioneers upon whose shoulders we are seated, who have gone before us and laid the foundations.

May our own shoulders be broad and sturdy enough to transport our descendants.

Our mission is to be thankful for yesterday, generous toward tomorrow, and caring today.

TWO HEARTS

"Great people have two hearts: one bleeds and the other forebears."

Kahlil Gibran

We must possess two hearts and use them as interchangeably as we would our right and left hands.

When friends are ill, they need us to weep with them amid fear and agony. They also covet individuals who can step aside from turmoil and be sturdy.

Our task is to keep both hearts ready, on call, for service to our kin.

LOOK FOR SURPRISES

A six-year-old girl had been getting up at the crack of dawn to "look for surprises".

"But you can't expect surprises every day," she was told. "They're only on birthdays, Easter and Christmas."

"That's not true," she replied. "When I looked out the window yesterday I was surprised by a daffodil. This morning I was surprised by a tulip."

The little ones shall lead us.

In the mid-nineteenth century, thinkers like Margaret Fuller, Walt Whitman, and Ralph Waldo Emerson contended that all of life was a miracle.

Religion previously considered miracles to resemble turning water into wine rather than the daily wonders of the natural world.

Why do we wait for supernatural interventions when earthly surprises lie before our very eyes?

BIRTHDAY OF LOVE

*"What matters today is not the difference
between those who believe and those who
do not believe, but the difference between
those who care and those who don't."*

Abbé Pire

Knowledge is secondary to loving.
Truth is the servant of compassion. The
foundation of any relationship is caring,
whether it be partner-to-partner, parent-
to-child, friend-to-friend.

With a groundfloor of active caring,
people become more interested in and
trusting of one another.

It is not knowledge, wealth, or
power but love that makes the world go
around meaningfully.

Let us make today another birthday
of love.

WHERE ARE WE GOALING?

"What good are strong and agile legs if we don't know in which direction to run?"

Michael Quoist

Many are those with strong bodies and sharp minds. Few exhibit purposeful spirits.

Our body and mind are rendered ineffectual without spiritual direction. "Without a vision, the people perish" proclaims the Old Testament.

A pilot, somewhere over the Pacific Ocean, cried out, "I'm lost, but I'm making record time!" Our culture applauds speed over direction. We have numbers of youth bounding over educational barriers at a rapid clip but with no notion about who they are or where they're going.

We need, early on, to help our children wrestle through the foundation questions: Who am I? Where am I headed? How can I best get there?

WHY ME?

As the waters of the Red Sea were parted, Moses said, "Why do I always have to go first?"

The oldest child in a family has a similar feeling when paving the way for younger siblings. So do offensive linemen on a football team as they block for running backs who follow behind them.

All of us, at one time or another, will be the first in line to face a crisis or take the risk. Moses was scared, but it worked out all right for him. It does for us too. We are seldom swallowed by the seas.

As Mark Twain quipped: "I am old and have known a great many troubles, but most of them never happened."

ALWAYS YOUNG FOR LIBERTY

When in 1830 William Ellery Channing (fifty years old at the time) was told by an acquaintance, "You seem to be the only *young* adult I know," Channing replied, "Always young for liberty, I trust."

We wrinkle and grow weary. Instead of trying to reverse inevitable physical processes, we need to remain young for things that truly matter: young for liberty, love, laughter, and learning.

There is no reason why we can't remain vigorous, youthful carriers of liberty all our lives.

April 21

PUBLIC AND PRIVATE VIRTUES

"Of course, it is possible to have both the public and the private virtues, but it seems rare: Byron ready to die for Greece, Shelley passionately engaged in the fight for human rights, Ruskin pledging his life and his fortune all made a pretty unattractive mess of their private lives."

Maisie Ward

People who choose public service often do so because of unhappiness at home. Yet I remain convinced that the full and good life includes tending to both our private and public spheres.

If we are giving too much as citizens and too little as partners or parents, then we need to redress the balance. Or vice versa.

Everyday we need to review our balance sheet.

LONG LOOKING

*"I recovered my tenderness by long
looking."*

Theodore Roethke

We are fatigued, jaded, brittle.
Where is the tenderness in our souls?

We bring it back by "long looking."

We look long at the beauty of a
foreign mountain or familiar face.

We look long at our choices and our
discardings.

We look long at our roots and our
wings.

We look long at our troubles as well
as those of our neighbors.

We look long at what previously
caught only quick glances.

Long-looking means quieting down
and taking our spiritual pulse.

THREE QUESTIONS

"All of us should learn before we die what we are running to and from and why."

James Thurber

We need to know where we are running in our lives. Toward fame, family prosperity, vocational security, or service to humanity? Or some combination of these? What is the fundamental purpose of our existence? What is our governing passion?

We are pulled and pushed in life. There are problems we are fleeing along with possibilities we are pursuing. What are some of the concerns we want to leave behind? Are our reasons for abandonment reasonable ones?

Finally, just why are we leaving certain things and traveling after others? Which *why* underlines our lives?

These questions occupy our lifetimes.

AWAY WITH PERFECTION!

"You, therefore, must be perfect, as God is perfect."

Matthew 5:48

I beg to differ with the Revised Standard Version translation of this New Testament passage.

The word *teleios* does not mean perfection but wholeness, finished-through, completion.

Too often religion demands the frantic, fruitless, pursuit of perfection. We clobber ourselves, as well as others, by seeking an elusive perfection. The truth is that perfection of any kind is impossible anywhere whereas improvement of every kind is possible everywhere.

Our aspiration should be to become whole persons whose bodies, minds, and spirits are co-ordinated—individuals who, recognizing our blemishes and flaws, try to transform them.

Three cheers for our faults, minor and major, those we've already shown and those, to quote Pogo, "we haven't even used yet."

ENOUGH, BUT NOT TOO MUCH

"The unexamined life isn't worth living."

Plato

We need to examine our lives—weigh, measure, and analyze where we've been and where we're going. Coasting is for those who wish to go downhill.

On the other hand, the over-examined life isn't living either. We aren't on earth to sit around and scrutinize ourselves to death. As the cartoon woefully notes: "Face it, Alice, analyzing our relationship *is* our relationship."

Examine *and* live. Ponder *and* do.

DIPLOMACY

> *"Diplomacy is the art of stepping on someone's shoes without spoiling the polish OR the art of jumping into troubled waters without making a splash."*
>
> Art Linkletter

Diplomacy is an art which needs careful practice both in family and community. Adroitness is essential everywhere.

We need to learn tact; that is, how to touch one another with firm, friendly, and fair hands. As Webster noted: "Diplomacy is the skill of handling events without arousing hostility."

We spend our entire lives learning how to be diplomatic—neither pushy nor pushovers.

BLOSSOMING

"I said to the almond tree: 'Sister, speak to me of God.' And the almond tree blossomed."

Nikos Kazantzakis

The almond tree was asked to speak of God. It responded in action. The closest we humans get to God is not through silence or talk, belief or prayer, but through deeds.

As Gandhi put it: "God appears to us not in person but in action."

Note the action of the almond tree. It is life affirming. It brings color, growth, beauty to its surroundings.

The almond tree, in "speaking" of God, does what it does best; it blossoms.

WINNING SOME VICTORIES

"It would be a shame to die without winning some victories for humanity."

Horace Mann

This is a reminder to stay active on the moral front, with small and big issues alike.

Mann knew that moral activists were often disappointed during our lifetimes. Therefore, we must keep faith and fight the good fight, day in and day out, in hopes of garnering "some victory for humanity."

The size of the triumph doesn't matter. That it enriches life on this planet does.

"Service is the rent we pay for the place we take up on earth."

THOUGHTS TO WORDS

"We know that he (the Prime Minister) has the gift of compressing the largest number of words into the smallest amount of thought."

Winston Churchill

One of my colleagues confessed that he wasn't the fanciest orator or ablest administrator. His strength was thoughtfulness.

He reflected, pondered, and weighed his ideas before offering them. I admired his depth. We nicknamed him "The Thinker."

He wasn't the brightest in our group. He wasn't an intellectual. He was an old-fashioned, deep-down thinker.

When Alex spoke, you knew he had done his homework.

You listened.

THE CRUCIAL FACTOR

"If we agree in neighborly love, there is no disagreement that can do us injury, but if we do not, then no agreement can do us any good."

Hosea Ballou

We celebrate Hosea Ballou's birthday today. This prominent preacher who promoted universal salvation and hope was born in 1771.

Ballou declared that love was the crucial factor in all situations. Love must be present whether we agree or disagree. Love enables us to grow, feel affirmed, be accepting of our neighbors, both in times of cooperation and of conflict.

Disagreements can hurt our egos, but they will do us no real harm when surrounded by the spirit of love.

Agreements may bolster egos, but they are of no benefit unless shored up by the presence of caring.

In all human encounters, love is the highest common denominator.

MAY

OF DREAMS AND VISIONS

"Your old people shall dream dreams,
your youth shall see visions."

Joel 2:28

Our culture endorses both dreams
and visions but glibly claims that the
former is the possession of the young
while the latter belongs to our elders.
The Bible urges us to consider that the
opposite can also be true.

It invites the older ones in our midst
to keep on dreaming. It reminds us that
we don't finish our fantasies in our
eighties. There may yet remain private
passions to explore. To retire is not to
turn in, to rust unburnished.

And "your youth shall see visions."
There is more to youth, even those with
only a decade under their belts, than
frantic activity and reckless dreams.
Children too see visions, have vision.

Our minds can be active from start
to close.

SWELL IMPERCEPTIBLY

"The buds swell imperceptibly without hurry or confusion, as if the short spring day were an eternity."

Henry David Thoreau

One little girl's description of nervousness is: "I feel in a hurry all over, but I can't get started!"

Nervousness, on the whole, is creative. We need an anxious edge to be productive. Problems come when we hurry into panic or confusion.

One place to experience creative, growth-producing passivity is in the natural world. Scrutinize the wonders of your garden or nearby park. Notice the changes, the growth which occurs without hurry.

In our human lives there is also a time to swell slowly, surely, "imperceptibly."

A PASSAGE

*"One today is worth two tomorrows; what
I am to be, I am now becoming."*

Benjamin Franklin

I count on today. "A bird in the hand
is worth two in the bush." I give all to the
present, which, in turn, will become
yesterday.

I prepare for tomorrow. I am not
waiting until I am sixty or eighty-five to
do something. I won't even remember
what it is when I arrive at those ages. Let
me be bold enough to be and do what I
most wish to be and do right now.

I am ever becoming who I am.

PROCRASTINATION

"Don't put off until tomorrow what you can put off until the day after tomorrow just as easily."

Mark Twain

Procrastination is more than a nasty habit.

It becomes a full-blown malaise, if left unattended. That's part of the double-bind for the procrastinator, who puts off doing anything, thus aggravating the problem.

Procrastinators should list the pay-offs received in postponing, then see if similar benefits can be garnered in better ways.

There is a scriptural fragment in Ecclesiasticus which makes a useful distinction: "Deliberating is not delaying."

SURPRISE

"There are radiance and glory in the darkness, could we but see, and to see, we have only to look."

Fra Giovanni 1513 A.D.

When we are buried in spiritual dark, there is nowhere to turn, no steps to take, nothing to view. We are lost in despondency. No radiance or glory is to be found.

But we often turn out to be our own worst culprit. We assume a fetal position in the dark. We close our eyes and hide.

When we are ready and able to do so, we might open our eyes and be surprised to behold shining beams of piercing radiance.

INFINITE SPACES

"It is impossible now even to imagine the levels of awareness of which we are capable. What we need are major efforts to explore inner as well as outer space."

Jean Houston

Blaise Pascal in *Pensees* says that "the eternal silence of these infinite spaces frightens me." Both our inner and outer spaces are infinite and frightening.

There are moments in our lives when our primary territory for searching-and-finding will be *outer* space and other times when our focus will be *inner* space.

Both are mysterious places worth visiting. We dare not evade facing the void and fullness of either realm.

TEN MINUTES TO LIVE

"This Book is dedicated to men and women across the country who love literature and give it their lives . . . these are the people who, if you told them the world would end in ten minutes, would try to decide, quickly, what to read."

Annie Dillard

If I were alloted ten minutes in which to live, I would spend them as follows. I would share *four* minutes with loved ones, *two* centering upon some thought from religious literature, *one* minute weeping, *two* in quiet confession and supplication, and my remaining moments in healing a broken situation.

How about you?

ABSCESSES

"Healthy, strong individuals ask for help when they need it, whether they have abscesses on their knees or in their souls."

Rona Barrett

We resist asking for help. We seek emotional support only in desperation. Consequently, we muddle into deeper trouble.

When our car doesn't work, we take it to the garage. When our roof is leaking, we phone a repair person immediately. When our head aches, we take the necessary measures. Yet when our spirits are wounded, we hesitate to ask for help in restoring them.

Strong people seek succor amid difficulties.

A MATTER OF PERSPECTIVE

"For one thing I have resolved not to castigate myself for not being a grownup. Instead of judging my life against, say, Mozart, who at my age was almost dead already, I will think hard about Gauguin, who at my age was still a banker."

Ellen Goodman

A small shrub growing next to tall pines looked at the ground and said, "Look how tall I am." The tall pine, looking toward the sky, sighed: "Look how short I am."

Comparisons are inevitable in life. We are slower than some and faster than others. We are more or less agile communicators depending upon the company we keep. We will be superior or inferior to someone, in some ways, somewhere, but it matters not.

We are called to be the irrepeatable persons we were created to be. Nothing more and nothing less.

SHIPS AT BUS STATIONS

"Everybody is waiting for their ship to come in...at the bus station."

Ron Clark

We live in an era when people are clamoring for rights and privileges. They believe there is a particular ship coming in with their name on it.

However, it appears that too many of us are waiting passively. We may obtain our ticket, but we sit around waiting for, rather than pursuing, results.

Sadly, when we muster the energy to do something about our destiny, we show up at the wrong point of embarkation.

We need to know where to start. We need to know where we're going. We need to have our ticket in hand. Then we need to move.

CENTER OF THE BEAM

"I began the day with Vaughn Williams'
Mass *sung by the King's College choir.
There are days when only religious music
will do. Under the light of eternity things,
the daily trivia, the daily frustrations, fall
away. It is all a matter of getting to the
center of the beam."*

May Sarton

George Leonard reminds us that
there are societies so primitive as to have
no apparel other than loin clothes, no
tool other than stick or stone, no
permanent dwelling, no carving or other
plastic art, "but nowhere on this planet
can you find a people without music and
dance."

Religious music enables my life to
reside "under the light of eternity." It
happens listening to Handel's *Messiah* or
wailing gospel songs.

Paying heed to my breathing, playing
the guitar, holding and being held by my
wife are other visits to the center of my
beam.

FULL—FLEDGED LOVERS

"...The Eskimos have fifty-two names for snow because it is important to them; there ought to be as many for love."

Margaret Atwood

General George Patton was asked: "What is the mission of the army?" "That's clear," he replied. "Ths mission of the military is to destroy the enemy. Are there any other questions?"

The same goes for religion. The mission of religion is clear: to be full-fledged lovers. Are there any other questions?

There are numerous ways of describing "love," at least fifty-two of them, but such complexity in naming need not derail us humans from our mission to become lovers.

A full-fledged lover is one who keeps growing and giving on all fronts: loving friends and family, those far and near, at work and at home, strangers, even foes. Loving is creating an affectional, caring bond that nourishes and enlarges both giver and receiver.

Our day's homework is laid out for us.

133

CROAKERS

"There are croakers in every country, always boding its ruin."

Benjamin Franklin

Pessimists abound. They are depressed and eager to take everyone else down with them. Frightened, they try to terrify others around them.

We need critics, but not croakers. Critics, at their best, pinpoint flaws in those realities which they cherish. Critics lament, but don't condemn. They perceive weaknesses **and** strengths. They urge changes, not just complaints. They don't bode ruin, they invite renovations.

HAVE A GOOD MOURNING

*"Blessed are those who mourn, for they
shall be comforted."*

Matthew 5:4

We receive comfort as a gracious,
unsolicited gift. We are comforted in
different ways. We are consoled from
unlikely sources. We are comforted when
we directly ask for it.

Jesus reminds us that we can also
be comforted when we dare to mourn,
weep our insides out. In the process of
grieving we cleanse our systems and are
strengthened. Catharsis leads to comfort.
Falling to pieces produces healing.

Often we choose to suppress our
hurt, go stoical, brave it through. Until
we grieve openly we are unable to
receive lasting relief.

THE DANGER OF PASSIVITY

"The chief sin of modern men with respect to their partners and children is not harshness, nor parsimony, not tyranny, not injustice or eccentricity but passivity."

Karl Menninger

Domestic violence, especially wife-battering and child abuse, is a monumental social problem.

Passivity presents a dilemma, too. Men get so wrapped up in work lives that we offer leftover emotional crumbs to our clans. We need to be more attentive in order to grow a caring family.

As women join the work force in greater numbers, they find themselves saddled with energy-loss. They are drained, too passive to give much to either partner or children.

Passivity has become a pervasive familial plight. We men and women need to help one another through it.

USE ALL YOUR LETTERS

"The alphabet of living is capable of forming a nearly infinite number of combinations, or situations. Yet some people have never acquired more than the spelling of one word: DITTO, reducing all singularity to commonness."

Abraham Heschel

We are master copiers and conformists.

We also have the talents needed to be unique and irrepeatable creatures.

We can pay serious heed to, even follow, others without mimicking them.

We need not turn into dittos.

RULE AND STAR

A scientist and minister are conversing. The scientist says, "I don't know much about religion, but I imagine it can be summed up in the golden rule." The pastor replies, "Well, I know little about science, but I assume it can be summed up in 'Twinkle, twinkle, little star...'"

Science and religion have long been adversaries. Each has oversimplified the other. This is changing.

Religious people are now empirically grounded, and scientists ackowledge the imprecision of their craft and the mystery of the universe. It is a healthy trend.

After all, cooperation, not combat, is the name of life.

THE WONDER OF SILENCE

*"Everything has its wonders, even dark-
ness and silence."*

Helen Keller

We are unduly nervous around
darkness and silence. We shine
flashlights into the dark rather than grow
accustomed to it.

We fill any silence of over thirty
seconds with noise.

One of the signs of maturity is
increased comfort living amid the dark
and silent periods of existence.

When Thomas Carlyle and Ralph
Waldo Emerson met for the first time and
realized the depth of their kinship, they
sat together without saying a word. They
simply enjoyed being with each other.
There was no need to chatter.

I'M FLEXIBLE

Malcolm X told a reporter in an interview that did not appear until after his death: "I'm big enough to tell you that I can't put my finger on exactly what my philosophy is now, but I'm flexible."

Malcolm X was born in Omaha, Nebraska this date in 1925. His life was cut short by a hail of assassin's bullets.

In his autobiography he wrote: "I do not expect to live long enough to read my book..." He who had grown up in a world of extremism and violence grew near the end of his remarkable life to feel that flexibility not dogmatism, love not hatred, was the heart of strength.

As he stated: "The true criterion of leadership is spiritual. We are attracted by spirit. By power we are forced. Love is engendered by spirit."

When I studied for the ministry two decades ago, the autobiography of Malcolm X was mandatory reading.

It still should be... for all sensitive citizens.

ON YOUR BOTTOM

"Even though you sit on the highest throne in the world, you still sit on your bottom."

Montaigne

Humility is the *bottom* line.

Everyone of us shares ignorance, simply on different subjects. We are frightened of one thing or another. None of us is exempt from the curse of gifts unoffered and hurts carelessly administered. Blotches stain the records of all human creatures.

Furthermore, we are seated upon the shoulders of those who have gone before us. The seat which is ours today is never entirely one of our making.

The table is a good place around which to gather: children and parents at a meal; negotiators at a summit conference; people playing cards for enjoyment. For around a table we start from the same position of being seated on our bottoms.

DEALING WITH THE DAILIES

"When I die, my epitaph should read: SHE
PAID HER BILLS. That's the story of my
private life."

Gloria Swanson

Here is an actress, producer, businesswoman reflecting upon her home life. There are exceptional dimensions and twists to most of our odysseys. But the heart of our lives has to do with how we play minor parts rather than major roles.

Deadlines. Details. Drudgery. Life is composed of all that. Life has to do with paying bills. On time.

A PLACE WITH A VIEW

"Maturity is a solid place with a view."

Vincent Sheean

Our wanderings in life are more successful if we operate from a home base. We need "solid places" in our lives: places of assured rest and sustenance, places to return to after racing all over town.

Our solid places need a view, lest we become claustrophobic or reclusive. The view opens up everything, including ourselves. It presents new horizons.

A solid place with a view marks the mature life.

CARING AND BEING CARED FOR

"In the sense in which we can ever be said to be at home in the world, we are home not through dominating or explaining or appreciating but through caring and being cared for."

Milton Mayeroff

Being at home in life is difficult at best, but only possible when we are engaged in cooperative rather than contentious activities.

There are moments when appreciating is the prime response. Explaining is valuable too; we dare not eschew our rationality. Even dominating has a role to play, if we think of dominating as the productive wielding of power.

We remain most naturally and fully at home in this universe through caring and being cared for. . .at home with self, with neighbor, with the ecosystem.

DIFFERENT ANGLES

*"We are at our human finest, dancing with
our minds when there are more choices
than two."*

Lewis Thomas

A teacher told his third grade pupils
about the chicken. "Isn't it wonderful,"
he exclaimed, "how little chickens get out
of their shells?" One of the eight-year
olds was moved to respond, "What beats
me is how they get in!"

Truth is kaleidoscopic. One person
sees one side of it; another perceives
another angle. An eight-year old is going
to experience a different marvel than we
adults.

We grow rich when all ages gather
together and swap our angles.

May
25   STORM WITHIN

"The wise one in the storm prays God, not for safety from danger, but for deliverance from fear. It is the storm within which endangers one, not the storm without."

Ralph Waldo Emerson

Emerson was born May 25, 1803. There is no more insightful philosopher, poet, and essayist in American history.

The wild storms within can be emotional ones. They can be rooted in our historical journeys. They can even grow from our imagination. Nonetheless, they rage.

The storms within cause the most damage in our lives. Fortunately, they are the ones about which we can do the most.

LIGHT WITHOUT AND WITHIN

*"May the blessing of light be upon you—
light without and light within."*

Irish blessing

There is light outside—sources of enlightenment and warmth which are beyond our making or control, yet nonetheless essential.

There is also light inside us— sources of power and insight residing in our hearts, though often disguised and underrated.

To be blessed by life's supply of light we need to receive radiance from both places.

A cartoon in *Punch* shows a woman praying at bedside: "Is there some way you could help me, Lord, but make it look like I did it all myself?"

The last thing we want to do, when we are in trouble, is ask for help, yet it is often the very thing we must do.

We need human help outside ourselves; we need divine support beyond humans.

NAME YOUR ANCHORS

*"One must not tie a ship to a single anchor,
nor life to a single hope."*

Epictetus

We give ourselves to just one cause,
one friend, one intention and when that
anchor fails, our life goes afloat.

There is no single hope that sustains
our life but a whole cluster of hopes.
Sometimes what serves as an anchor at
one time fades into the background;
others emerge.

Anchors are crucial, but there is
more than one available in our universe.
Name three that shore up your present
existence.

THE WAY TO BE BLESSED

"Do you think you can take over the universe and improve it? I do not believe it can be done. The universe is sacred. You cannot improve it. If you try to change it, you will ruin it. If you try to hold it, you will lose it."

Lao Tsu

In Taoism the goal is the recovery of the primordial harmony of heaven and earth. This is not achieved by intervention in the world, either human or subhuman, but by befriending the universe.

As George Foot Moore notes: "Not to bring the universe, by activities of any kind, into harmony with our desires, but by creative quietude to be in harmony with the universe, is the way to be blessed."

Our charge is to live in accord with the laws and rhythms of the cosmos rather than amend them.

JUST KEEP BREATHING

A woman celebrating her 100th birthday was interviewed on television. The anchorperson asked, "To what do you owe your longevity?" "Nothing to it," the woman replied. "Anybody can do it. I just keep breathing."

Breathing is the heart of life. It is the bridge from body to mind. It builds up the lungs, strengthens the blood, and revitalizes every organ in the body.

Alan Watts used to say that the curious thing about breath is that it can be looked at both as a voluntary and involuntary action. I am doing it, *and* it is happening to me.

It reminds us that there is no hard and fast division between what we do and what happens to us.

Breathe and let breathe!

CLEAR AND NEAR

"The word is very near you; it is in your mouth and in your heart; so that you can do it."

Deuteronomy 30:14

We already know enough. We are well aware that love of self, neighbor, natural world, and God comprise the imperatives of the spiritual trek. These commandments are nestled in our interiors.

Life is filled with mysteries beyond our awareness. Life is also filled with mandates "very near you...in your mouth and in your heart."

We are to bow before the one and obey the other.

HUMOR IS COUNTERBALANCE

"After a little of Einstein there ought to be a little of Cole Porter, after talk about Kierkegaard and Kafka should come imitations of Ed Wynn and Fields. Humor is counterbalance. Laughter need not be cut out of anything since it improves everything. The power that created the poodle, the platypus, and people has an integrated sense of both comedy and tragedy."

James Thurber

It takes comedy and tragedy to produce the full life. While sadness usually comes univited, we need to occasion our laughter. We have to grow our funny bones.

Studies show that working comedians are more depressed than average persons but also possess superior ego strength. Laugh-makers seem to have the emotional ability to convert despondency into creative material.

Charles Lindner, humorist, said: "A person has two legs and one sense of humor, and if you're faced with the choice, it's better to lose a leg."

JUNE

AM I NOT THEIR LEADER?

"The one who cannot obey, cannot command."

Benjamin Franklin

Good leaders know how to be good followers.

The unthreatened leader is willing to be under the power and authority of another. As Benjamin Disraeli (1804–1881) put it: "I must follow the people. Am I not their leader?"

We need public officials who exemplify Disraeli's attitude, who practice good leading and following.

DREAMS WORTH
DOING...NOW

"Hold fast to dreams, for if dreams die, life is a broken-winged bird that cannot fly."

Langston Hughes

Name your aspirations and dreams. Some are unrealizable; accept them as such, let them go quietly. Others are achievable but not significant enough to hold fast. You may revisit them later, but for now, let them also pass.

Which dreams remain? Which ones are for the world, for your loves ones, or pertain solely to you? What do you plan to do with them?

Do something toward actualizing one dream in this coming day.

Major accomplishments begin in minor ways.

NEVER ENOUGH

"One never loves enough."

Aldous Huxley

There are kinds of "love" to avoid. The smothering kind. The guilt-inducing variety. The passive-aggressive sort. The conditional version. The sloppy, syrupy kinds. Perhaps these types don't even merit the name of love.

Love when it is non-possessive, when it enhances the being of both giver and receiver, when it builds bridges and deepens bonds, is always welcome. There will never be an oversupply of such love.

Sometimes I look at my wife, parents, children, friends, and I am moved to utter: "I can never love you enough!"

THE GOOD LIFE

"Keep me away from the wisdom which does not cry, the philosophy which does not laugh, and the greatness which does not bow before children."

Kahlil Gibran

When we cry, we are visiting our depths.

Our philosophizing becomes jaded if it isn't sprinkled with foolishness and laughter.

Finally, look at all the humanitarians in history. Most could get down on their knees, next to little folk, and share eyeball to eyeball, the learnings of their hearts.

It's hard to improve upon this summary of the good life.

A WHY

"They who have a why to live . . . can bear without almost any how."

Nietzsche

When we realize where we want to travel during our lifetimes, then it is a matter of turning on the engine and motoring there.

Yet we can't answer all the *why*'s of reality. Sometimes we come up empty in our searching, and we still have to muddle along.

Then, blessedly, we figure out another *why* amid our daily grind, and we forge ahead.

TRY DILIGENCE

"Everything yields to diligence."

Antiphanes

There are things we cannot accomplish no matter how hard we try. The right conditions are not present. We don't have the ability.

Nevertheless, diligence, perseverance, hard work do pay off. Corny or not, I tell our children that life is a matter of 10% inspiration and 90% perspiration. I remind them that triumph translates as try+umph.

I want our children to drive hard without being driven.

Diligence doesn't bank on good moods, reasonable conditions, confident feelings. Diligence relies on itself—diligence.

As first rule, last resort, and middle path...try diligence.

SOMETHING FOR ME TO DO

"In a world where there is so much to be done, I felt strongly impressed that there must be something for me to do."

Dorothea Dix

Motivated and sustained by her faith, Dix set out to reform the treatment of prisoners and mentally ill.

Many people are paralyzed by the prophetic vision. Because we cannot do everything, we do nothing. Or we attempt something in haphazard fashion and burn out.

Dorothea Dix focused her compassion. She avoided the modern malaise of activities: cause jumping. She devoted herself to one specific task of improving the environment for prisoners and mentally ill in our land.

Lucy Stone phrases it accurately: "I think God rarely gives to one person more than one great moral victory to win."

CONSECRATED CHICKEN SOUP

"It is not the nature of the task but its consecration that is the vital thing."

Martin Buber

Any job can be boring or worthless. It brings us joy when consecrated.

When will we learn that meaning lies not in something but in what we bring to that something? You and I are meaning-makers.

Novelist J. D. Salinger has Zooey say to sister Franny that no prayer is going to save her until she can recognize consecrated as different from concentrated chicken soup. The difference lies in how the water is added, how it is heated, and how it is served.

It is the act of making concentrated chicken soup into consecrated chicken soup which blesses both the one who prepares and the one who consumes.

Today is my mother's birthday. She has consecrated my life.

FOREVER NAMELESS— FOREVER FELT

"Forever nameless, forever unknown, forever unconceived, forever unrepresented yet forever felt in the soul."

D. H. Lawrence

This concept of God is similar to Taoist philosophy or passages from Hindu scriptures. It also resonates with references to deity in the Old Testament like: "I am who I am."

Lawrence doesn't pretend to understand, let alone capture, God. But his lack of intellectual certitude does not imply absence, for God is "forever felt in the soul."

I, too, sense God profoundly sometimes, but words fail me in such moments.

FIFTEEN YEARS OLDER

"To me, old age is always fifteen years older than I am."

Bernard Baruch

This thought rings true whether we are five, thirty, or sixty-five.

I admire the Gray Panther's button: "How dare you presume that I would rather be younger!" Consider Joshua Slocum, who set out at fifty-one to sail around the world alone and made it three years later.

Handel, who was deeply in debt and recovering from a stroke, at fifty-seven accepted a commission to write a choral work for a charitable performance and produced The Messiah.

Edith Hamilton, who did not even begin her work as a mythographer until she had retired from teaching at sixty, inaugurated a series of four annual trips to Europe when she was ninety.

We would be wise when we are thirty-five to be the best thirty-five we can be rather than yearning to be twenty or worrying about when we will reach fifty.

LUSTING FOR KNOWLEDGE

"I should like to go on forever learning. I lust for knowledge..."

Aldous Huxley

Those were the words of Huxley as he was leaving Oxford.

Note he didn't want to live forever; he wanted to go on forever learning.

We often say "thirst and hunger" after knowledge. I like the term "lust" better. Our thirst and hunger are sated at some point, but bona fide lusting is unfillable. We keep on lusting.

Our job as parents and teachers is to light fires, to get our offspring to burn with desire for wisdom, to be hot with it all their lives.

A CHUNKY LIFE

"There's enough space in the day for a lot of things. I like to have big chunks of solitude and big chunks of people."

Annie Dillard

Dillard has the unerring ability to create interludes of palpable stillness in her writing. Her passages encourage us to imagine ourselves resting in serene, natural settings.

Some of us have little pieces of solitude and huge slices of humanity on our agendas. Or vice versa.

The balanced existence mandates a substantial dose of both apartness and togetherness.

BACKWARDS AND FORWARDS

"Life must be understood backwards. But it must be lived forwards."

Soren Kierkegaard

We need to remember the blunder we committed back in March of 1974 so that we won't repeat it. December of 1958 was a painful time to endure; let us learn from it. The special joy we experienced in the summer of 1937 has energized us for a long time.

But we are entering never-before hours and are invited to live today resourcefully. If we don't grow from the mistakes of yesterday we are likely to revisit them. Likewise, if we don't learn from the wisdoms of yesterday, we are prone to forget them.

We need to understand and appreciate where we have been before we set out on new paths.

FIVE WORDS OF HOPE

"There is no lost good."

Dorothy Day

In Jewish literature there are many tales about the struggles of the *zaddikim*. This term is usually translated as "the righteous" but actually means "those who have stood the test."

The zaddikim were set apart not because of position or reputation so much as because they wrestled, day in and day out, with evil in pursuit of the good and emerged scathed but with their characters intact.

We become cynical as we age. We condemn the messiness of politics. We downgrade the school system. We rail against immorality.

Religion reminds us that "there is no lost good." Every moment spent in compassion, every cent contributed to justice, every effort given to peace reaps dividends.

Goodness was a lifelong calling for the zaddikim.

REAL GENEROSITY

"Real generosity toward the future lies in giving our all to the present."

Albert Camus

We parents seldom think of generosity to our children in terms of giving time and love here and now. We put aside money or momentos for our children with plans to parcel them out at a later date.

The reality is that our offspring need our nourishment, discipline, and gifts daily.

It is unwise to postpone our generosity. Being spiritual tightwads now and lavish givers tomorrow doesn't make sense.

OMISSIONS

"We are morally responsible for every wrong which we have the power to prevent."

J. D. Jones

There is a rabbinical saying: "We will have to give account on the judgment day of every good thing which we might have enjoyed and did not."

Morality is often seen as a code of prohibitions, which, if obeyed, secure entrance into heaven. Truth is larger and the ethical life tougher than that.

One can resist negative behaviors and still fall short of a good life. We must be as concerned with our omissions as with our commissions.

There is nothing that Jesus makes more clear than the tragedy of neglected opportunity. "And the door was shut" were sobering words that greeted the five women in the New Testament story who neglected to put oil in their lamps.

CHANGE SPEEDS

"If they try to rush me, I always say, I've only got one other speed—and it's slower."

Glenn Ford

Speed rules. We are hares in a hurry from morning until night. But when I feel driven, it is usually I who am in the driver's seat.

Brenda Ueland says:

"Our imagination needs moodling— long, inefficient, happy idling, dawdling, and puttering."

Remember that Jesus spent thirty years in preparation for three years of ministry. Many of us take a mere three years of preparation for a thirty-year career.

I need to slow down, be still, change speeds.

Perhaps you do, too.

STILL CARRYING HER?

On one occasion Tanzan was traveling with another monk, Ekido, down a muddy road, where they met a beautiful woman in a fine silk kimono, unable to cross the intersection.

Lifting her in his arms, Tanzan carried her across the road. Ekido did not speak to Tanzan until they reached a lodging temple that night, when he finally exploded angrily: "Monks do not go near females, especially young and lovely ones!"

"I left the woman there at the crossroads," replied Tanzan simply. "Are you still carrying her?"

This Buddhist story has ostensibly to do with monks' relationships with women. It has more to do with our letting things go rather than clinging onto them, things that hinder forward movement like resentments and fantasies, jealousies and anxieties.

There are certain emotions which burden our spirit, weigh us down, keep us from traveling ahead.

We need to leave them back at the crossroads.

ORGANIZE GOODNESS

"Five of you shall chase a hundred, and a hundred of you shall chase ten thousand."

Leviticus 26:8

We live in an era of self-sufficiency. Some people believe that by banding together, they will be diminished. Others contend that groups are superfluous.

The ancient Hebrews realized the importance of sharing crises and multiplying joy. Evil is often organized; so too must goodness be. We increase our effectiveness by joining in solidarity with like-minded spirits.

Leviticus predicts that while five of us can interact with one hundred (twenty times more), a hundred of us will engage ten thousand (one hundred times more).

AN UNSUNG COMPANION

"I never found the companion that was so companionable as solitude."

Henry David Thoreau

We meet different companions along life's trek—people, animals, books, activities, feelings, crises. Life grows wearisome if we only pursue one or two kinds of companions.

Thoreau invites us to retreat in order to greet an unsung companion: our selves.

Spend quiet, quality moments alone today. Be still and affirm your interior. You may be growing a new and essential friendship.

THE GIRAFFE

"It is only by risking ourselves from one hour to another that we live at all."

William James

The Giraffe Society honors people who stick their necks out and defy the spread of mediocrity and indifference.

If everyone of us would dare to make contributions to changing our world, there wouldn't be a need for such an organization.

Giraffes stand tall, proud, above the crowd. They are endangered by the insensitivities of humankind, as are we all.

Giraffes are also gentle and peace loving.

BEYOND SELF-LOVE

"To be whole, we have to serve greater causes. We are like horses. Horses have to draw wagons to grow their whole potential. They cannot live for themselves alone. We have to serve others, but be free to do it in our own way."

I. F. Stone

Staring at our own navels should help us realize our irrevocable connection with larger humanity. A hazard occurs when we try to find ourselves solely within ourselves.

We must live for causes which include our gifts yet transcend our egos.

This challenge might prove unbearable if we were coerced to pursue service in the same manner. This isn't the case in America. We are free to choose our own obligations.

A LOVER'S QUARREL

"And were an epitaph to be my story, I'd have a short one ready for my own. I would have written of me on my stone: I had a lover's quarrel with the world."

Robert Frost

We children of the universe are called to fight fairly with those realities we cherish.

It is healthy to argue and struggle with parents, offspring, our faith, and dreams rather than cut ties with them.

Fights can refine our commitments.

Loving and conflict belong together.

THE UNCONVINCIBLES

"It is impossible to reason people out of something they have not been reasoned into."

Dean Swift

Everyday we run into unconvincibles. They are people who have obtained their opinions on an emotional basis and cannot be reached on a rational one. It is prudent not to argue with extremists. You end up hurling invectives.

Once a great throng of people collected about the Rabbi of Apt to hear his teachings. "That won't help you," he cried to them. "Those who are to hear, will hear even at a distance; those who are not to hear, will not hear no matter how near they come."

Spiritual pioneers are committed to the open, not empty, mind. We change our minds too. But trying to mix seriously with persons of closed minds is a fruitless venture.

In Grandma's memorable phrase: we might as well save our breath to cool our porridge.

TINY PUSHES

"I know who I was when I got up this morning, but I must have been changed several times since then."

Lewis Carroll

The passive voice isn't sufficient. We change (active voice) ourselves from morning to night. If it is evening, reflect upon the day to locate moments when you felt yourself shifting gears, undergoing a change.

If it is morning, be aware of upcoming alterations in your life.

Take with you this thought of Helen Keller:

"The world is moved not only by mighty shoves of the heroes and heroines but also by the aggregate of tiny pushes of each honest wonder."

A SPLENDID THING

"Traditions are a splendid thing; but we should create traditions, not live by them."

Franz Marc

Traditions are helpful, if we know when to grow beyond them.

Sometimes we cling to conventions we should ignore, drop, or pass on. Traditions are to serve us and not the other way around.

Traditions are those customs and rituals that transfer from others' hands into ours. After we have handled them with care and sensitivity, even molded them, then they move on to the hands of yet another.

TROUBLE IS A PART

"Trouble is a part of your life, and if you don't share it, you don't give the person who loves you chance to love you enough."

Dinah Shore

Some friendships never grow beyond the happiness zone. They remain giddy and superficial, facing neither anger nor grief.

Such relationships, while comfortable, never tap the deeper regions where troubles are faced and frustrations shared.

It hurts to be alive; it hurts doubly to love. Pain comes with the territory of caring about another. A loving bond creates ongoing wounds along with the caresses.

In loving I open my arms and heart to your troubles.

SMOOTH WAVES

"Speak tenderly to Jerusalem."

Isaiah 40:2

Soft-spoken and mild-mannered, the American bishop Bernardin has a knack for achieving goals without causing rancor. Says a top Catholic clergy in admiration: "When Bernardin makes waves, they're always smooth."

A teacher of mine in seminary said that there will be times in ministry when you must share painful, abrasive truths. Do so in gentle fashion. I have never forgotten that advice, whether sitting across from a parishioner, my wife, a community activist, or our children.

It is wise to speak softly when saying something harsh. As Gibran phrased it: "If you must be candid, be candid beautifully."

TEACHERS

*"Each gave me something for my journey:
a phrase, a wink, an enigma, and I was
able to continue."*

Elie Wiesel

There have been teachers who
nudged and yanked me farther along my
path.

I don't only refer to classroom
conductors. I also salute neighbors,
coaches, relatives, ministers, and peers
without whom my journey would have
been less instructive and inspirational.

Without these companions I might
not have continued the trip.

BURY NOT YOUR INTELLECTS

"So precious a talent as intellect never was given to be wrapt in a napkin and buried in the earth."

Angelina Grimke

Grimke was a nineteenth century American abolitionist, writer, feminist, and reformer.

Each of us possesses a different yet keen intellect. As a society we need to endorse the entire scope of intellectual power: the rational, the mechanical, the aesthetic, the spiritual.

As Will Rogers quipped: "Everyone of us is ignorant, only on different subjects." We need to be patient with ourselves and one another, for we are all likely, at any moment, in our own fashion, to be brilliant.

JULY

TWO AND ONE

"We have two ears and only one tongue in order that we may hear more and speak less."

Diogenes

Communication demands both sharing and listening. The art of hearing seems more difficult to sustain. That is why we grew two ears instead of one.

To be a good, responsive listener is to be about as passive as a good surgeon. Steady, reflective, quiet but hardly passive.

Listen to the speech of others. Listen even more to their silences. Listen to the subtle sounds of their beings.

Jacob Trapp phrases it: "If it is language that makes us human, one half of language is to listen." Silence can exist without speech, but speech cannot live without silence.

IMPROVISING

"Life is like playing a violin in public and learning the instrument as one goes on."

Samuel Butler

There are situations when we can practice our instruments in private or even obtain lessons on the side, but most of the time we are musicians improvising on the public stage of life.

I think predestination is a dreadful doctrine. I wouldn't want a fixed musical score to follow. I appreciate the fact that we humans can edit and adapt throughout the flow of our existence.

We were born for improvisation.

SERENDIPITY

"Serendipity: the gift of finding valuable or agreeable things not sought for..."

Webster

As a child I would ransack through trash cans and hunt for useless keys to put in my ever-expanding collection of treasures.

I might not locate a key, but my hands would run into a red ball which, while hardly new, could be squeezed to build up my wrists for sports. Serendipity! I was looking for one prize, and I found another along the way.

Have you ever found valuable things which have been lost by others? Have you made new friends while mingling with old ones? Have you been trafficking with an idea and met another one in the process?

CONVICTIONS AND PREJUDICES

"The difference between a conviction and a prejudice is that you can explain a conviction without getting angry."

Samuel Butler

When I get heated up, dogmatic, virulent about one of my viewpoints, I am harboring a prejudice.

My convictions are those opinions and commitments which I can share straightforwardly, even passionately, but free of hostility. My convictions come from my head as well as my heart. They are spirited *and* rational.

Convictions lend themselves to conversation; prejudices hanker for conversion.

This distinction is worth pondering in the political sphere as we Americans celebrate our country's birthday.

THE LAST STEP

"Ally yourself with time. It is the last step that counts."

Sainte-Beuve

As long as we live, there will be opportunities to restore a fractured relationship, heal an unforgiven situation, pursue an unrealized dream. Always one more chance.

We are a yearning species. Plodding to the finish line enables us to accomplish amazing results.

There is no better way to enjoy the journey than to treat each step as if it might be our last one.

INDIVISIBLE

"Freedom is an indivisible word. If we want to enjoy it, and fight for it, we must be prepared to extend it to everyone."

Wendell Willkie

Freedom isn't alone in being indivisible. Justice can't be given to some and withheld from others. Love doesn't work if we try to cut up pieces here and there like a birthday cake.

When we divide values, we can't help but show partiality and stir up strife among recipients.

Recall some of the indivisible virtues in your existence.

TRIFLES

"A word, a look, an accent, may affect the destiny not only of individuals but of nations. They are bold who call anything a trifle."

Andrew Carnegie

Bold isn't the word I would use here. Arrogant or foolish seems more to the point.

Expansive lives are lived by those who treat trifles as crucial. They dignify details. They play minor parts with major enthusiasm.

They treat every word, look, and accent with respect. They know that any given moment may turn life around, and they want to be present when it happens.

STAYING AROUND TOWN

"I have traveled a good deal in Concord."
Henry David Thoreau

"I have traveled widely in Roanoke, Virginia."
Annie Dillard

An expert is someone who lives fifty miles out of town. One of our own tribe speaks from the podium, and we hardly take notice. A visiting guru arrives, and we frantically take notes. As Jesus remarked, "Prophets are not without honor except in their own country and in their own houses." (Matthew 13:57)

Thoreau and Dillard spent a lot of time strolling about their home neighborhoods. They are encouraging us to know our own surroundings intimately before we rush to take tours abroad.

There is so much to learn at home, so much of beauty and worth available in our own backyards. We don't have to leave town to experience growth.

Something to think about this summer.

WHAT IS SOUL?

*"What is soul? It's like electricity. We don't
know what it is, but it's a force that can
light a room."*

Ray Charles

In our technologically sophisticated
age we measure an array of realities. We
graph them. We put them on screens.

Thank goodness we are unable to
quantify all the experiences of life. We
feel love, but we cannot objectify it.
There is evidence of trust in our
existence, but we cannot prove it. We
talk about soul, but we get foggy trying to
pin it down.

Both technology *and* mystery
enhance life.

WHICH WITH WHOM?

*"It is the duty of the press to comfort the
afflicted and to afflict the comfortable."*

H. L. Mencken

It is also the mission of government
and families to heed Mencken's counsel.

It is our highest human task to
support one another in sorrow and goad
one another in complacency.

Both jobs need doing. The art is
knowing when to do which with whom,
because the needs shift in our lives.

SOIL YOUR SPIRIT

"You are so afraid of losing your moral sense that you are not willing to take it through anything more dangerous than a mud-puddle."

Gertrude Stein

The only way to stay clean is to stay clear of the messy ethical struggles confronting sensitive humans daily. Life dares people to soil, scuff, and sully their spiritual outfits.

Good ballplayers get dirty. They don't play dirty; they dirty their uniforms because of the fairness of aggressive moves.

There is a time to stay in the dugouts, safe from the contest, but, sooner or later, the game of life must be played on the field, where the dirt is.

MARRIED TO CREATION

"Well, if one loves one's partner and one's children, after a while you begin to feel very close to God—not that your partner is God or the child is God but you're married to still one more aspect of creation, whatever it is. That is, you touch God."

Norman Mailer

There are various ways of missing or making connection with God. We spend our lifetime doing both.

We have a far better chance of communing with the divine if we love the creation fiercely and thoroughly.

Marrying is a good word here. It reminds us to commit ourselves to the created order with enduring respect and abiding affection, for better or worse.

Partners and children are high priorities in our marrying, but they aren't the only primary connections we must make during our odyssey.

DELIVER MY BEST SELF

"I've had a generous share of the good things, money, prizes. I lack for nothing. What I would like to do in the time I have left is deliver my best self."

John Updike

Updike doesn't ask to deliver a perfect self. He is not interested in becoming someone else, particularly at this juncture in his career. He would be satisfied to deliver his finest self.

You can't beat that for a life challenge.

A MOTTO

There is a slogan which served as the family motto of Bishop John A.T. Robinson from England: "non nobis solum sed toti mundo nati" (Not for ourselves alone but for the whole world are we born).

I can't think of a more fitting motto to pose in the halls of our homes. It catches the purpose of our birth, the mission of our family endeavor.

Loving ourselves is fundamental, but there is more. Our call is to serve the world with gladness, to share riches and resources beyond the walls of our private abodes.

FOREVER BIRTHING

"We can never be born enough."

e. e. cummings

There is being once born. There is being twice born. Mature spirituality claims that "we can never be born enough."

Great human beings are not born the first time or the second time. They evolve into degrees of near-greatness.

Outstanding persons in all spheres of life are willing to be born yet one more time.

OUT OF SIGHT, OUT OF MIND

*"I call it the Toilet Assumption—namely,
the notion that unwanted matter and
unwanted difficulties will disappear if they
are removed from our field of vision..."*

Philip Slater

We are prone to decrease the
visibility of social, ethical, and emotional
problems. Out of sight, out of mind is our
attitude.

We move through life according to
the "toilet assumption." Yet there remain
in our pasts things that haunt us and hurt
others until we face them. There are also
unpleasant tasks in our current lives,
which, if postponed, ignored, or flushed,
will cause grief in our tomorrows.

Spend moments today recalling
those events, things, people, challenges,
unfinished issues which, while out of
sight, should not be out of mind.

Be willing to invite one or two back
into your consciousness for honest and
healing encounter.

ON EARTH TO SHARE

"If you have knowledge, let others light their candles at it."

Margaret Fuller

If we are lucky enough to inherit or acquire wisdom, it is our obligation to share it at home and abroad.

We moderns are proud, possessive, even paranoid about our gifts. We horde rather than share.

Think of those pioneers who have paved the way for us. When we realize how many of our candles have been lit at the knowledge of others, we will rush to serve others.

Generosity grows in relation to gratitude.

DAMN NEAR IMPOSSIBLE

"It is easy to say no all the time, it is easy to say yes all the time, it is damn near impossible to be a parent."

Ric Masten

The toughest times in parenting are when we deal with gray areas, the "could-be" zones. There are moments when an appealing case can be made for either side of the struggle. Honest parenting requires a yes-no reponse: yes to one portion and no to another.

Our children mature when they start to answer our questions with less certitude than before, when "I'm not sure's" creep into their responses. For it's equally "damn near impossible" to be a child growing up in today's society.

May parents and children learn to share the courage of our confusions as well as our convictions.

GOES AHEAD

"Creativity is what cannot wait, cannot stop, cannot backstep: faster or slower, it always goes ahead—through, alongside, above, regardless of crises or systems."

Jose Rodrigues Migueis

Creativity moves inexorably forward.

I recall the creative people in my life. They are a few strides out ahead. They move their way through the wild and tangled brush that obstructs the more cowardly among us. They are willing to go ahead, even if it spells personal danger.

We need creative ones in every generation.

Call in the pacesetters.

As Lois Platford notes: "You have all eternity to be cautious in when you're dead."

TWO TESTS

"The test of courage comes when we are in the minority. The test of tolerance comes when we are in the majority."

Ralph Sockman

Courage and tolerance are like our left and right hands. We use them both to be full persons.

When we are in the minority, we are prone to display indignation and when we reside in the majority, we exude arrogance. Those two attitudes get us nowhere. They cause interpersonal deadends.

Measure yourself by the two tests above, and you will stay in superior spiritual shape.

THE VOICE WITHIN

"The more faithfully you listen to the voice within you, the better you will hear what is sounding outside."

Dag Hammarskjöld

Our lives are polluted by an incessant stream of noise. We are inundated by a cacaphony of sounds.

We need to visit what the Old Testament calls the "still, small voice" within our spirits.

William Sloane Coffin has said if average Americans knocked on the door of their own hearts, they would find nobody at home.

We cannot dialogue with each other until we are at home with ourselves.

OUR DIFFICULT TIMES

"This time is difficult. Wait for me. We will live it out vividly. Give me your small hand: we will rise and suffer, we will feel, we will rejoice...So let our difficult time stand up to infinity with four hands and four eyes."

Pablo Neruda

Neruda, the brilliant Chilean poet and activist, was the winner of the 1971 Nobel Prize for Literature.

He reminds us that we need one another especially during our difficult moments. Alone we are never quite as sturdy and resilient as when we share the gift of our "small hands." Lovers, parents, children, workmates, religious kin: we all need to band together in caring alliance.

To "stand up to infinity" will call upon us to join hands and eyes, spirits and minds. We need to make these difficult times a bit less difficult.

Our cries of pain and tears of joy are all better when shared.

IN GESTURES

"Being holy is majoring in love."

Dorothy Donnelly

I think of the father in Luke's gospel who forgave his prodigal son in gestures. He *clasped* him in his arms. He *kissed* him tenderly. He *gave* him gifts.

In another story, Zacchaeus was confident of God's forgiveness when Jesus *visited* his house.

These examples show us that love only comes alive in action.

In its truest form, love loves.

TREATMENT OF DISEASE

"The physician's task is to cure rarely, relieve often, and comfort always."

Oliver Wendell Holmes

Years ago I received treatment for mushrooming skin cancer which threatened my eyesight.

A specialist in Los Angeles performed the necessary surgical work four mornings in a row to save my right eye. He was methodical, professional, skilled. He was also cold, aloof, ornery upon occasion.

I wouldn't have traded his expertise for all the warmth in the world. I needed his savvy more than his sentiment. Yet, those of us in the healing arts can be both skilled and sensitive, impersonal and personal in proper rhythm. Our training needs to include learning how to cure, relieve, and comfort.

PERFECTLY USELESS WORK

Leonard Woolf, in the fifth volume of his autobiography, at age eighty-eight, looked back over fifty-seven years of political work and concluded: "I must have ground through between one hundred and fifty thousand and two hundred thousand hours of perfectly useless work."

Studious laborers put in more useless hours than the average worker, because they put in more total hours.

One of my life goals is to persevere when inspiration is absent or drive is flagging. There are the plodding and the spectacular. I prefer to be numbered among the plodders.

Thomas Edison, after failing to make a breakthrough in one of his experiments, was asked why he didn't quit. He said: "Well, I've found several hundred things that don't work. I'm on my way. Triumph may be around the corner."

THE ETERNAL NOW

"Do what you can, with what you have, where you are."

Theodore Roosevelt

The *can* has to do with outside limits, the *have* with innate capacity, the *are* with present location. Limits, capacity, and location are equally significant ingredients in one's commitment to action.

But notice Roosevelt's first word: DO. He doesn't allow for weasling, postponing, fleeing. DO!

Roosevelt is urging us to quit waiting until we are persuaded beyond a shadow of a doubt about a course of action, because that time never arrives.

There is a folk saying that goes:

"Nothing will be done until everyone is convinced that something ought to be done and when everyone is convinced, it's time to do something else."

LOVE LINKS

"The supreme experience of life is to share profound thought and then to touch."

William Butler Yeats

Thought and touch are hallmarks of human communion. The order in which they appear doesn't matter.

Sometimes we engage in deep conversation, then our bodies commune. Other times we move from physical contact to intellectual dialogue.

Spiritual wellness hungers for both thought and touch, touch and thought. . . all the day through.

FABLE

Jean de LaFontaine tells the fable about an old farmer who, realizing that he is about to die, calls his sons to his deathbed to tell them that his own parents buried a treasure somewhere on his land. Although he does not know where the treasure is buried, he assures his sons that:

"If each of you will search for it with hardihood, you are sure to find it."

The sons follow their father's advice, do not find any treasure, but work the land so thoroughly that it produces larger and larger crops thus fulfilling the father's final words: "If you would find a fortune, work hard."

Love, justice, community, and other life goals are, in one sense, never reached; yet if we are lucky and labor diligently, they may be found along the way.

TOUCH WITHOUT CLINGING

In a New Testament story Mary Magdalene, who loved Jesus very much, is said to have seen him after his resurrection, and she immediately ran to him. And Jesus said, "Do not touch me," but the Greek word *hatir* means "to cling to." In effect, Jesus said, "Don't cling to me, Mary!"

Don't cling to anything of the spirit. Don't cling to water, because the more you grab it the faster it will slip through your fingers. Don't cling to your breath; you will get purple in the face and suffocate. You have to let your breath out. That's an act of faith, to breathe out, believing that your breath will come back.

The religious pilgrimage is the art of knowing how to touch without clinging, of knowing when to accept and when to relinquish.

CHANGE OVER CHANCE

"Unless we change directions, we will end up where we are directed."

Confucius

Few of us regularly evaluate the directions of our journey. We leave things to happenstance. We allow external forces to play ping-pong with our fate.

The good life is a matter of activating change rather than submitting to chance. We are co-creators of the earth's future.

This is a moral mandate and a personal opportunity.

Robert Frost was once interviewed by a newspaper reporter and asked if he believed our nation had much of a future. The poet replied, "My friend, our founding forebears didn't believe in the future; they believed the future in!"

You and I are summoned to be change-agents rather than chance-takers.

NO STRINGS ATTACHED

"Persons who love us have invited us outside."

Bernard Cooke

When someone loves us, we are not only given something, we are enabled to give in return. We are "invited outside," outside ourselves, outside into the scarey openness of exchange, even intimacy.

Love invites us outside. It does not coax, pressure, or manipulate us. It simply invites.

Sometimes we turn the invitation down.

A strong, secure, sensitive love keeps on inviting in the hope that the loved one will someday R.S.V.P. in the affirmative.

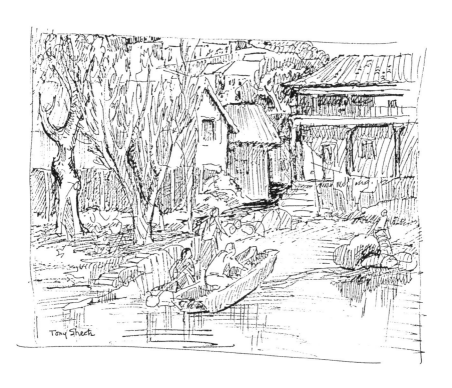

Tony Shech

AUGUST

SPREAD SOME SHINING

"My greatest joy was to spread a page with shining."

John Steinbeck

I have heard artists make a similar commitment when they declare: "My objective is to spread a canvas with vitality." Helping professionals remark: "If I can spread a face with new joy, my job has been done."

Everyone of us, in our own ways, can spread each day with a little wonder, hope, and love.

T.T.T.

"Put up in a place where it's easy to see the cryptic admonishment T.T.T. When you feel how slowly you climb, it's well to remember that Things Take Time."

Piet Hein

The Danish cartoonist, Piet Hein, has produced books full of grooks like the one above.

Things do take time. There is no trickier art to master than patience and waiting. Ponder places in your life that exhort you to be patient, take ample time. Remember: not only things take time, so do people, relationships.

There is a different twist to this grook. Things take time, people take time, work takes time, TV takes time, meditation takes time...there are many experiences in our lives clamoring for our limited moments.

Which are taking up the bulk of my time?

I am in charge of who and what fills the time slots in my existence.

SELF OR SCENE?

"Very often a change of self is needed more than a change of scene."

A. C. Benson

People move, switch partners, change jobs, swap friends in hopes of personal regeneration.

Few of us make internal shifts, because changing one's self is difficult, time consuming, painful.

Our tendency is to alter everything but our own habits, perceptions, biases.

We would like to make our aches go away with minimal effort.

A BLEND

"Grace is proportionate to exertion."

Sathya Sai Baba

Religion salutes, with equal fervor, both sides of the spiritual paradox: faith and good works.

We are blessed with moments of grace, graciousness, and gracefulness— all beyond our deserving. Our very existence is unearned.

On the other hand, those who exert will be in a receptive zone for the arrival of grace.

STRONG NOT NOISY

One thing the Merchant Marines learned during World War II, while traveling in convoys, was that the horn that toots the loudest is usually the one that's in the fog.

When I am lost in any kind of mist, I turn blustery. When I am insecure, I toot loudly.

On the other hand, when I am firm yet flexible in my convictions, I am gentler to both self and others.

We are called to state our faith with peaceful strength. Our voices and lives don't have to blare in order to display power.

KNOWLEDGE IS A MEANS

"You don't preach knowledge. You use knowledge to preach."

Martin Luther King, Jr.

Dorothy Canfield Fisher, the novelist, used to say that the college degree should be granted only ten years after the customary graduation day, on the basis of the graduate's performance as citizen, professional, parent, partner.

Maybe ten years is too soon. Perhaps when we are in mid-life is the time when our learning can be fairly assessed.

Education *per se* means little. It must result in fruits of maturity.

We learn in order to be more decent people. We acquire skills not to flaunt them but to use them in service. All of King's studies (and he received a doctorate in philosophy) enhanced his labors in the vineyard of social justice.

STARTING EVEN

A sergeant asks his cavalry recruits: "Have any of you ridden a horse before?" "No, sir," they all replied! "Well, then, the horses haven't been ridden yet either, so you will be starting out even!"

Someone has been there before us and is willing to pass on tips. We sit at the feet of parents, who, for better or worse, have paved many a pathway.

Sometimes though, in our relationships, we explore feelings or behaviors for the first time together. Or we create a project which has never been done quite like we propose to do it.

It is scarey to ride a wild, unbroken horse.

New directions in the interpersonal and vocational realms can be equally frightening.

And worthwhile.

OPTIMISM

"Anyone who writes a book, however gloomy its message may be, is necessarily an optimist. If the pessimists really believed what they were saying there would be no point in saying it."

John Robinson

Full-fledged pessimists stew in their own juices of negativism.

However, giving vent to frustrations, writing about upsets, demonstrating according to angers are creative ways of dispersing the gloom.

Winston Churchill figured it didn't make much sense to be anything but an optimist. I have always called myself a chastened optimist, but an optimist nonetheless.

I am not about to turn my life over to doom or gloom.

REGRETS

"Make the most of your regrets. To regret deeply is to live afresh.

Henry David Thoreau

Living with regrets stymies us. It resembles a "sour grapes" attitude or a driving-the-car-with-the-brakes-on approach to life.

Yet Thoreau has a point. Regrets can be motivating. Childhood losses can be converted to mid-life gains or sadnesses of young adulthood to breakthroughs during our sunset years. It takes re-membering and courage.

Regrets become debilitating when we focus on them without moving beyond them. They contaminate our lives when we forget, even repress, instead of confronting them.

I now see where I could become a better friend with some of my regrets and "live afresh."

POSTPONING

*"I find that before you retire you promise
yourself to do all sorts of things, but a great
part of your time is taken up with putting
them off and eventually you devise a
system of putting things off that takes up
all your time."*

Sir Sydney Smith

There is a time to ponder matters,
even postpone them. We all have a "wait
until later" folder, drawer or basket.
Some things need to gestate.

Nonetheless, some of us get into
bad habits, even ruts; "putting things off"
becomes a way of being.

We figure out inventive ways to
keep from doing things which must be
done.

Procrastination can take up most of
our waking hours.

MERRYMAKERS

"And Elijah said to Berokah, 'These two will also share in the world to come.' Berokah then asked them, 'What is your occupation?' They replied, 'We are merrymakers. When we see people downhearted, we cheer them up.'"

Talmud

There is no greater calling than to be a merrymaker, a bringer of joy into the depressed corners of existence.

Comedians are generally sad people off stage. Conversely, some plaintive leaders in society are comical in their private lives. They would be better off if they displayed laughter in their public lives.

May our occupation be merrymaking, at home and abroad.

WE ARE MESSENGERS

"There is no rest for a messenger 'til the message is delivered."

Joseph Conrad

Messages of anger, affection, and thankfulness cause unrest until we deliver them to the right address.

Some understandably must remain unexpressed. There is wisdom in the aphorism: "To say the right thing at the right time, keep still most of the time."

However, we harbor thoughts and feelings which need to reach their destination. We know the difference. Do we have the bravery to deliver our messages, including the painful ones?

Before it's too late.

GROWERS UNITED!

"Only the persons who understand and appreciate what it is to grow, who understand and try to satisfy their own needs for growth, can properly understand and appreciate growth in another..."

Milton Mayeroff

It takes one grower to appreciate another one.

If we are growing in our work, then we are more able to empathize with others who are moving along in their profession. How we are growing will differ; that we are growing is shared in common.

Such a bond is germane to friends and lovers. For intimacy to deepen, each individual must be growing as well as the partnership itself. The primary reason for broken relationships is that the parties involved grow apart or grow at radically different speeds.

HAVING ENOUGH HEART

"...the physical survival of the human race depends on a radical change of the human heart."

Erich Fromm

Einstein said, upon the unveiling of the atomic bomb, that as our technological skills have matured, so must the resources of our hearts.

Radical changes have occurred in every area of our political, social, and scientific lives. To keep pace our hearts must deepen and broaden, open to the ways of compassion.

The word "courage" comes from the same stem as the French word "coeur" meaning "heart." Our survival as the human species depends on our showing courage and having heart.

I am struck by the poignance of the concern voiced in Ezekiel (18:31): "Turn around! Why do you want to die?"

GIVEN FREELY EACH DAY

"What will you have when you finally have me? Nothing. Nothing I have not already given freely each day I spent not waiting for you but living."

Michelle Murray

When friends came together for a memorial service for Michelle Murray, they read one of her works called "Death Poem" that contains today's centering thought.

Memorial services should be celebrations of the gifts and goofs, the strange grandeur of this irrepeatable human being. Open caskets won't bring us closer to the person. Murray goes on to write: "You will have my fingers but not what they touched."

A poignant reminder to exchange love, insight, joy, and hurt with the person who has died, before he or she dies.

MISSING THE POINT

"Vengeance is not the point; change is."

Barbara Demming

This is hard counsel for a society which majors in getting ahead, back, and even.

In partnerships, we are set on vengeance rather than change. We seek to score points rather than make the game more humane. The same pattern obtains in the business world and in political organizations. Even religious communities and families are not exempt from the disease of retaliation.

Vengeance is a dead end; both sides lose.

**August
17**   **THREE CONVERSIONS**

*"A person needs three conversions: first of
the heart, then head, finally, of the purse."*

Martin Luther

I like Luther's order.

A presentation is reasonable and
convincing. But that's not enough to
change us. Little happens when our head
is filled but our heart remains unmoved.
We need to be inspired to behave
differently.

Finally, action is required. One
mode of action in our social order is
putting our cash where our mouth, head,
and heart are. Money is liquid power.
Check stubs display our deepest choices.

Heart, head, and purse, these three,
are intertwined.

SAVE FACE—LOSE SELF

"Masks, then, allow people to sace face, but to lose self."

Richard Lessor

There are times to wear masks. It is neither possible nor desirable to be naked in all our interpersonal encounters. We cannot be uncovered all the time.

But a mask that becomes a fixture erodes our identity. We slowly but surely lose our character. We become addicted to roles, to phoniness.

Wear masks discreetly, whether at home or in public.

LET THE CORNS HEAL

"Don't step on the same toes two times in a row; let the corns heal!"

John Baker

Sometimes we are relentless in voicing our viewpoint. We harp away endlessly, riding our hobby horses. As leaders we "railroad."

We are more effective as parents and professionals when we change pace, vary our interpersonal moves— sometimes come on strong, other times recede, always be gentle.

GEE, YOU ARE YOU

"Guru is spelled gee, you are you!"

Jean Houston

People have traveled the world over in search of a guru only to learn the desired wisdom resides within their hearts.

The most valuable gurus drive us not to our knees but push us back into self-discovery.

Our call on earth is to fulfill ourselves rather than imitate masters.

DESPITE THE EVIDENCE

"We should all have one person who knows how to bless us despite the evidence."

Phyllis Theroux

We need a friend, partner, parent, counselor, minister to whom we can go and say: "Here I am, blemishes, holes, and all—accept me!" That is the essence of the Prodigal Son story.

The younger son squanders his inheritance, ashamedly returns, and "while he is yet at a distance," physically afar and psychologically marred, the son is accepted by his father.

He is accepted contrary to any earnings, despite any evidence. The prodigal son is blessed and made worthy by the love of the father.

In truth, the father becomes prodigal too, that is, lavish and overflowing in love.

HERE'S MY RELIGION

*"If you want to know what my religion is,
come and see me operate."*

Clinton Lee Scott

People who pontificate via platitudes
are a dime a dozen. They fill street
corners and air waves, even airports.

Religious and pious people are not
the same. Religious individuals have their
public and private worlds match. There is
congruence between how they spend
their time, money, and talents. Their
parental, partnering, and professional
lives mesh.

The way to authenticate another's
life is to spend time together.

LESSONS

"Teach us to care and not to care. Teach us to lie still, even among these rocks."

T. S. Eliot

There are times we show care for others. There are moments to quit worrying about something, to back off, not to care.

In between these two extremes is the skill of lying quiet and still, neither moving forward or away, being present, waiting.

We have chances everyday to practice all three lessons, even among the rocks.

EXISTENCE AND LIFE

"Just to be is a blessing; just to live is holy."

Abraham Heschel

What an unspeakable joy to exist in this universe! Our existence is a blessing beyond our asking, earning, or power.

Living transcends existence. It demands a conscious decision on our parts to select a certain quality of existence. Living means being with vitality and fullness. As Jonathan Swift penned: "May we live all the days of our lives."

Being is a blessing. Living is holy.

RESERVE A NOOK

"...leave a little fallow corner in your heart ready for any seed the winds may bring, and reserve a nook of shadow for the passing bird; keep a place in your heart for the unexpected guests, an altar for the unknown God."

Henri Amiel

We are prone to cage wonder and package mystery.

We experience an exquisite sunset and grab our camera rather than ingest its grandeur. We even run out and sell our photograph to a magazine.

Mystery, when nourished, thrives in our moments of intimacy and excellence, solitariness and worship, song and dance.

Let "unexpected guests" enter your life.

PURSUING EXCELLENCE

"The one education which amounts to anything is learning how to do something well; whether it is to make a bookcase or write a book."

Willa Cather

Certain subjects have come easily and comfortably to our son, Russ. Spanish was not one of them.

He and I worked incessantly on that very subject. We did so not only to see what we might produce through diligence but, more importantly, to pick up the tools of discipline and perseverance.

Russ never became proficient at Spanish, but he has become excellent at living as he moves into adulthood.

The folksinger Bob Dylan used to say: "I would like to do something worthwhile like perhaps plant a tree on the ocean, but I'm just a guitar player." There should be tree planters *and* guitar players, for few of us will be versatile enough to excel at both.

Our charge, while on earth, is to find our gift, explore it, then exhibit it.

Our humanity is wasted when we fantasize or try to be someone other than who we really are.

239

A DROP OF HONEY

"A drop of honey catches more flies than a gallon of gall."

Abraham Lincoln

There is a time to be confrontive, even abrasive. Situations go unsettled when we grow weak-kneed or resort to sentimentality.

Lincoln's advice holds us in good stead. He always felt, and rightly so, that we win people over through "unassuming persuasion."

WAKE UP!

Nearing death, Buddha was asked by Ananda for his secret doctrine to be passed on.

Buddha is reported to have said, "There is no secret doctrine. There is wisdom to be found, but you must find it for yourself."

The genius of Buddha's thought centers on his conviction that only you can save yourself, or move toward salvation, for we never reach our spiritual destination.

The name Buddha means "an awakened one." Note *an* not *the* awakened one. It is from the Sanskrit root *budh* "To fathom a depth, to penetrate to the bottom, to perceive, to come to one's senses, to wake."

Buddhism begins with a person who shook off the daze, the doze of life's fog, who woke up.

The challenge of pumping spiritual iron is to be awake—awake to sorrow and joy, new truths and ancient learnings, self-fulfillment and service...to be awake, awake, awake.

GREATEST OUT OF THE SMALLEST

"Live your life while you have it. Life is a splendid gift. There is nothing small in it, for the greatest things grow by God's law out of the smallest."

Florence Nightingale

If we believe something is irrelevant, we treat it that way. We have minimal expectations for that project. We don't bank on a particular child doing much of worth.

However, if we are expectant, if we pay ample attention to the small— surprising results can happen.

Who among us has not experienced mustard seed miracles in our lives?

Nan-chuan said: "Your body is unusually big; isn't your straw hat too small?" And Huang-po replied: "Though my hat be small, the entire universe is within it."

Small is not always beautiful, but it can contain entire worlds within its tiny grasp.

ANTAGONISTS

"Have you not learned great lessons from those who dispute the passage with you?"

Walt Whitman

We tend to read only those ideas which we approve. We join mutual admiration societies. Yet we grow most when grappling with notions at odds with our own.

One of my professors assigned us an essay on a philosophical adversary. Our task was to pinpoint the real, not just paper, strengths of our opponent and determine how her or his viewpoint could shape our own.

Listening long and hard to the merits of our antagonists rids our minds of excessive bias.

ONESIMUS

"Formerly he was useless to you, but now he is indeed useful (Onesimus) to you and to me."

Philemon

This book of the Bible is skipped over, being only ¾ of a page long, nestled between Titus and Hebrews.

It tells the story of Paul, while in prison, befriending a runaway named Onesimus. Paul feels so strongly that Onesimus has turned his life around that he helps him out of confinement.

He states that Onesimus was formerly *useless* but now is *useful.* The very name Onesimus in Greek means "useful." When he became true to his real being and purpose in life, Onesimus became useful to one and all.

The same is true for us. When we pursue not somebody else's identity but our own, then—and only then—are we valuable contributors to existence.

SEPTEMBER

A RECIPE

*"Give all your nights to the study of
Talmud and by day practice shooting from
the hip."*

Irving Layton

The title of this brief poem by
Layton is "Recipe for a Long and Happy
Life."

I am not convinced that these words
are a recipe for a long and happy life.
Happier, probably; lengthier, if we're
fortunate. Nonetheless, it remains sound
advice.

Our purpose as human beings is to
study our heads off, be it during the day
or night, then put our books aside, and
live naturally.

BETWEEN THOUSANDS AND THOUSANDS

"Our lives oscillate not merely between two poles, such as the body and the spirit, the saint and the sinner, but between thousands and thousands."

Herman Hesse

Some people operate in a world of certitudes. They see things in terms of black and white, regularly choosing one over the other.

Other individuals are more comfortable amid ambiguity. Things may appear black or white to them, but one time they choose black, the next time white.

Still others of us, including Hesse, perceive life to be a continuum with multiple shades of black and white with which to confuse us and from which to choose.

There isn't just one choice, or even two, but many, every morning we climb out of bed.

AMBIDEXTROUS

*"To brave people, good and bad luck are
like a right and left hand. They use both."*

St. Catherine

You and I must be flexible enough to
handle the trials and triumphs that
happen in our lives.

Bravery is interior strength. We
can't predict what forces will strike our
lives from the outside. We use whatever
fortune comes our way.

Many of us cater to the natural hand
and shy away from our minor one. We
turn to our places of power and avoid
our weaknesses.

The brave among us employ both
hands.

LOVE CONSISTS IN THIS

*"Love consists in this: that two solitudes
protect and touch and greet each other."*

Rainer Maria Rilke

First, we come to a love relationship
from solitude, the serenity and strength
of our aloneness. If we are uncomfortable
being ourselves by ourselves, then we are
probably rushing into intimacy.

Second, we shield and comfort one
another in a partnership. We can over-
protect or under-protect. Simply *protect*
is sound counsel.

Third, touch is mandatory.
Emotional and spiritual connection are
necessary but insufficient. Physical
connection is essential in love.

Finally, we greet one another not
once or twice but again and again. There
is freshness in the love encounter. Each
meeting is virginal.

YOU AIN'T GOT THE MELODY

"As Mark Twain once retorted after his wife repeated verbatim a redolent string of cusswords he had just uttered: 'You've got the words Livy, but you ain't got the melody!'"

David Johnson

No matter how hard we try to imitate the behavior or verbal outpouring of another, we just can't do it.

Our children try to follow in our footsteps but would be better walking in their own shoes.

The melodies we know best are our own.

DIFFERENT STROKES FOR DIFFERENT FOLKS

"Do not do unto others as you would they should do unto you. Their tastes may be different."

George Bernard Shaw

The trouble with the Golden Rule is that it is a partial wisdom.

It speaks to the general human need to be treated fairly, but our personal situations vary greatly. There are certain things I like to give or receive that might be alien to your spiritual diet. Our partnerships must heed the particulars of our tastes rather than be slavish to rules.

We remain exceptional creatures.

JUGGLING THREE ACTS

"See everything, overlook a great deal, correct a little."

Pope John XXIII

Life invites us to juggle three acts.

We need to "see everything": be alert and available to life's flow.

We need to "overlook a great deal": be magnanimous, forgiving.

Finally, we need to "correct a little": offer only advice that will improve conditions.

There is an old Latin proverb:

*"In things essential, unity,
"in things doubtful, liberty,
in all things, charity."*

September 8

LIMITS OF LOVE

"The essence of being human is that, in the brief moment we exist on this spinning planet, we can love some persons and some things..."

Rollo May

We are encouraged to love *some* persons and *some* things, not everyone and everything.

Love makes judgments; love is discriminating; love is limited. Lavished at large, in the abstract, love becomes sentimentalized and irrelevant.

Love is not an idealized form; it is an actualized encounter with real people.

WALK BESIDE ME

*"Don't walk in front of me—
    I may not follow.
Don't walk behind me—
    I may not lead.
Walk beside me—
    and just be my friend."*

Albert Camus

There are moments to lead *and* times to follow. Nevertheless, real friendship finds people sharing alongside most frequently.

As the legend goes, we were born not from the foot or head of Adam but from the ribs so that man and woman would not be over or under one another but side by side.

BEYOND LETHARGY

Dorothy Parker, when told Calvin Coolidge was dead, remarked, "How can they tell?"

Such satire is an apt description of various notables in society as well as many of life's ordinary folk. "Walking moribundity" is a common malaise in our culture. It pertains to people who are zombie-like or flat in spiritual tone.

An avid student rushed to his Hasidic master one day and shouted excitedly, "Rabbi, I went through the whole Torah this week!" Whereupon the Rabbi replied, "Yes, but how much of the Torah went through you?"

The prime way to combat lethargy is to pursue projects of moral weight, to create beauty beyond our own appearance, and to display love beyond our own gratification.

The Torah must go through us!

September 11   FLY IN FORMATION

"Geese fly in formation. They have a seventy percent advantage over a single goose seeking to do his or her 'own thing'. Put simply, geese fly much faster in formation than one by one."

Browne Barr

We are rounding the bend from an epoch of self-centeredness. We now know that the self is fulfilled not by itself but through service beyond itself.

We are beginning to salute commitment, community, and covenant as a society.

We are recognizing that to soar boldly and effectively we must fly in formation.

Just as stray or lost geese circle about, we are often lost for several days in a fog, until we hear the familiar honking of the flock.

ABUSE IS USE WITHOUT GRACE

"Abuse is use without grace."

St. Augustine

Over the centuries we have abused our environment. We have used the resources of our ecosystem without thought or care. We have been ungracious to our kin, the earth.

We are beginning to affirm the organic view that we are part of an entire web, and if part is broken or torn, the whole web shudders.

We are of the soil, of the sea, of the air. We are related to and are a product of nature.

As the Indian proverb goes:

"The frog does not drink up the pond in which it lives."

**September
13 REBIRTH**

*"To suffer one's death and to be reborn is
not easy."*

Fritz Perls

We are always rehearsing for our
death.

When we say farewell to a job and
start a new one, we are dying and being
reborn.

When we move out of one intimate
bond and enter the world of aloneness,
we are repeating the death-rebirth cycle.

When we relinquish certain dreams
and face life without specific hopes, we
suffer a painful rite of passage.

This dying and rebirthing flow is
never easy, but it keeps us in spiritual
shape for our final goodbye.

A CRITICAL MASS

"There isn't time to wait with bated breath for the formation of a 51% majority. A 'critical mass' will do the job."

Mark Satin

We need not wait for a fifty-one percent majority of people to be converted in order to make the world more humane, merciful, and just. A critical mass is adequate to start the job. A number of concerned and committed people can move a congregation, a community, a continent, a cosmos.

What constitutes a critical mass? Estimates range all the way from two to twenty-five percent.

Let's join forces with the gentle, caring ones and save our planet. Let us associate with the critical mass of humans who treat the *uni*-verse as one.

LOAVES AND HYACINTHS

*"If thou of fortune be bereft and in thy
store there be but left two loaves; sell one,
and with the dole buy hyacinths to feed thy
soul."*

James T. White

Life entails both.

When we are able, we are called to
lift the sadness of our neighbor and raise
our own spirits, engage in compassion
and bask in beauty.

An existence which does only one or
the other is a lopsided venture.

Loaves and hyacinths, hyacinths and
loaves.

Albert Camus put it similarly:

*"There is beauty and there are the
humiliated. Whatever difficulties the
enterprise may present, I would like
never to be unfaithful either to the
one or the other."*

CREATIVE STRADDLING

A young teacher appeared for his first job interview in a rustic mountain village. Members of the school board quizzed him thoroughly on the acceptability of his views for teaching their youngsters.

At last one elder asked, "We hear a lot of talk about the world being round, while others reckon that it appears to be flat. How do you feel about this?"

The man, anxious for employment, replied, "Why, I can teach it either way!"

In decision-making, we must take a leap of faith beyond the scoreboard of pluses and minuses. But before we leap, we need to sort out the issues.

Being able to teach it either way, or creative straddling, makes us more accepting individuals. We know the negatives in our own decisions and the positives in the options we turned down.

It keeps us tolerant and balanced.

THE PATH IS THE GOAL

St. Catherine of Siena spent three years in silent meditation and emerged with the conviction: "All the way to Heaven is Heaven."

Heaven isn't something to be attained later and elsewhere; it is reality to be experienced and embodied here and now.

Peace isn't some abstract destination; it is an immediate pathway.

If we aren't creating and receiving joy daily, then we won't recognize, let alone appreciate, joy at some future date.

FIRES IN COLD ROOMS

A biographer once said of a stateswoman: "She lit so many fires in cold rooms." That is a standard to which we all might aspire. If we have the warmth of love within, we ignite many a worthwhile blaze.

There are ample cold rooms in which to practice—at work or home, publicly or privately, all our lives.

When it is our turn to be memorialized, may someone say, above all else, Susan or Jack lit fires in cold rooms.

WHEN WE LAUGH AND SING

"When we laugh and sing, we are blest by everything; everything we look upon is blest."

William Butler Yeats

Laughing and singing are paths to blessedness.

When I complain, scowl, or retaliate, I am caught in the clutches of cursedness. I am miles from blessing self or anything.

When I laugh, life giggles and shakes in delight.

When I sing, everyone is less interested in lamenting or harming.

WE WORK IN THE DARK

*"We work in the dark—we do what we
can—we give what we have. Our doubt is
our passion, and our passion is our task."*

Henry James

There are moments when we are
enlightened, matters seem clear, and we
share a measure of certitude.

Usually, we labor amid insecurity,
we sculpt with inadequate materials, we
work in the dark.

Yet I don't take this to be a
pessimistic message at all. Through dark
and doubt, "we do what we can—we give
what we have."

Given the limits of our human
condition, the results of our labors are
marvelous.

COMMA IN AND COMMA OUT

*" I spent all morning putting in a comma
and all afternoon taking it out."*

Oscar Wilde

Writing is rewriting what we have
already rewritten. Occasionally, it's
worse; we have literary constipation, not
even a comma emerges.

No one who has ever seen a writer
trying to join passion, clarity, and verve
with an accurate selection from the
eleven million words in the English
language could fail to appreciate the
excruciating labor involved. As Paul
Engle remarked: "Before anything else,
a work of art is WORK."

I once asked my father-in-law, an
artist of the highest order, the innocent
question: "How long, Millard, did it take
you to paint that particular painting?"
"Seventy plus years!" he calmly replied.

A lifetime is not too long a span in
which to seize possession of our visions
and express them with power.

IS OUR HELPING HELPFUL?

Part of the spiritual life is to be a servant, a helper.

We do not, however, need "helpers" of the kind described in one of Virginia Glascow's novels: "She loved to help others. You could tell the others by their hunted look."

Or as it is put in Taoism: "Am I helping others because they need help, or do they need help because I'm helping them?"

We need to take stock of our helping motives. When we are driven, manipulative, or foster dependencies, our help is counterproductive for all.

Our serving needs to liberate rather than enslave.

FOOTING

*"That's the first thing that got me about
this place, there wasn't anybody laughing.
I haven't heard a real laugh since I came
through that door...When you lose your
laugh, you lose your footing."*

Ken Kesey

These words were uttered by
Randall Patrick McMurphy in Kesey's
novel about life in a mental hospital,
entitled *One Flew Over the Cuckoo's
Nest*.

Because of the level of depression
and pain in such institutions a heavy dose
of laughter is sorely needed. Through
laughter, inner torments work
themselves out. It is the medicine needed
to revive a wracked heart or withering
spirit.

We need sure footing along life's
rugged paths. A steady supply of laughter
gives us footing.

September 24

I CHOOSE ALL OF ME

"My humanness is decreased when I exclude any part of me."

Barry Stevens

I turned corners in my growing when I owned up to portions of my being which were unfortunate, unpleasant, downright mean.

The spiritual challenge is to grow wholeness not perfection. The perfection-seeker prunes and polishes, frantically trying to present a purified face to the world.

Whole individuals merge yin and yang. They affirm the interrelatedness of their qualities. They believe that personhood is diminished when cleansed of shadows and demons.

The old saying, "some are characters while others have character," is a shallow aphorism. Some of the very dimensions that make me a character dare not be relinquished.

We must affirm our garbage as well as our goodness.

THE BATTLE OF BEING

*"The funniest mortals and the kindest are
those who are most aware of the battle of
being."*

W. H. Auden

Simply being is a struggle
sometimes. Becoming is even more of a
battle for us humans. We are placed on
earth not only to be "aware of the battle"
but to be engaged in it.

We cannot enjoy the luxury of being
spectators in life's fray. Spiritual sides are
drawn. The moral enterprise is a partisan
struggle. We need to stand up and be
counted for what we believe and cherish.

Rugged competitors of life are
usually funnier and kinder than
fencesitters.

WORTH REPEATING

"Everything important has already been said. But no one was listening, so it must be said again."

André Gide

Occasionally, we do some original things, but in the weightier matters of love, justice, and mercy, the saints have all been there before us.

I don't take this to mean that we should merely salute our saintly forebears and not do good deeds ourselves.

Decency is worth repeating ad infinitum. Someone, somewhere, will see or hear its worth for the first time.

PEACE BE WITH YOU

The first words spoken to his disciples by Jesus, the Prince of Peace, after his resurrection were: "Peace be with you." (John 20:20)

We will never prove to be credible mediators of love and peace to others unless we harbor a sense of peace within ourselves.

Activists tend to race out to effect global peace and fail to grow serenity in their gardens.

Politicians rant and rave about justice in our land and embody inequality in their own domiciles.

Although we cannot wait until we have total inner peacefulness before we declare and pursue it abroad, some interior tranquility is a necessity or our public displays lack authenticity.

Peace be with and within us all.

FINDING TRUTH

"The terrible thing about the quest for truth is that you find it."

Remy de Gourmont

We search for new truths and visit old ones. We remain on this expedition all our days.

Some people only seek; they never find.

There are emotional and physical truths, moral and intellectual ones; nonetheless, there are abundant truths in existence to find, and then, to embody.

Our spiritual depth is measured by what we do in life with what we have and what we discover.

THE GOAT IS GONE

*"For I have learned, in whatsoever state I
am, therewith to be content. I know both
how to be abased, and I know how to
abound..."*
St. Paul

A woman went to her therapist for
advice. "Doctor, our situation is terrible.
There are nine of us living in one room,
and we can't get along. It's awful. What
shall we do?" The counselor thought
about it a while and then said: "Get
yourselves a goat and keep it in the room
with you." The woman was puzzled but
promised to do as she had been told.

A week later she came back more
desperate than ever. "Doctor, things are
worse than before. All of us and that goat,
it's unthinkable. We can't stand it
anymore."

"Ah, yes," said the therapist. "Well,
then, you can get rid of the goat."

Two days later the woman came
back—beaming, this time. "Everything is
wonderful. The goat is gone, and we are
so happy. It's just the nine of us now!"

There are always situations better
and worse than our current one. It is wise
to live well with what we have and who we
are.

DEVILS AND ANGELS

*"If my devils are to leave me, I am afraid
my angels will take flight as well."*

Rainer Maria Rilke

Rilke wrote these words in
withdrawing from psychotherapy after
learning the goals to which it aspired. I
share the same anxiety Rilke did,
although I favor therapy that helps us
confront ourselves.

Devils and angels are intermingled in
the best of us. Good therapy does not
flush our devils. It helps us utilize their
energy in constructive ways.

Another way to put it, according to
Abraham Lincoln: "It has been my
experience that folks who have no vices
have very few virtues."

OCTOBER

October 1   A COMFORTER FROM SORROW

*"There is no space wider than that of grief.
There is no universe like that which bleeds."*

Pablo Neruda

At a recent exhibit of American quilts at the Oakland Art Museum an artist fashioned from her husband's clothes a tableau of their life together and entitled it "Widow's Quilt." Around certain scenes—their wedding day, the gravestone of a child—her usually meticulous patching veered. The uneven stitches formed a powerful metaphor for her grief.

By assembling from the fabric of memory all that had been lost, all she still cherished, she created a comforter of warmth for others and a work of enduring beauty.

A FRESH START

> *"Love has no awareness of merit or demerit. It does not seek to balance giving and receiving. Love loves."*

Howard Thurman

Justice records merits and demerits. Propriety balances giving and receiving. There is nothing wrong with either justice or propriety. A civilized society needs both.

Nevertheless, a relationship or group that knows only equality or etiquette is incomplete without the permeating presence of love.

Love is generous beyond score-cards. Love forgives inequities. Love is needed when the bottom line is either catastrophic or garbled.

Love loves.

COPING WITH ROADBLOCKS

"When life loses its meaning and the soul is aware of its sickness, the alternatives are breakdown or a fresh and perhaps deeper look at oneself and reality."

Allegra Stewart

One way of looking at life is to read it as a series of roadblocks. Chinese has two characters for the word "crisis": one meaning *danger* and the other *opportunity*. In life we come to a roadblock and we are challenged to push it aside, climb over it, or be paralyzed in its presence.

There are minor and major roadblocks. Some are immoveable without the combined efforts of inner fortitude and outer help. Some hound us for months; others can be transcended in a matter of moments. In any case, we can rest assured that there will be additional roadblocks up ahead.

The quality of our earthly existence is determined by how nimbly we handle our daily roadblocks.

NEIGHBORS AS OURSELVES

*"We really love our neighbors as ourselves.
We hate others when we hate ourselves.
We forgive others when we forgive
ourselves."*

Eric Hoffer

It is true that how we feel about and
treat ourselves shows up in our interpersonal encounters.

The same happens for nations.
When we are insecure with our own
ideals, we tend to be distrustful of other
countries. If we could begin to honor
peace and justice in our own backyard,
we would be far less obsessed with
waging war in someone else's.

**October
5**   **AN ARTIST FOREVER**

"Every child is an artist. The problem is how to remain an artist once you grow up."

Pablo Picasso

Today is Pablo Picasso's birthday. This world famous Spanish painter was born in 1881.

We begin life with the spontaneous urge to share ourselves. For the most part, before report cards arrive, we are unabashed in our artistic imagination.

Paul Signac said of Monet: "He paints as a bird sings." We aren't all Monets, but we can continue all our days to express ourselves naturally.

We are not simply created beings or parts of the universe. We are partners in the ongoing creation.

We live not so much where we breathe as where we create.

PLAYFULNESS

"In the form and function of play, our consciousness that we are embedded in a sacred order of things finds its first, highest and holiest expression."

John Huizinga

A little pro-fun-ditty.

Today is the anniversary (1857) of the first important chess tournament held in the United States. Games enrich and balance our lives.

I learned Backgammon and Hearts recently and revived my passion for the card game Rook as well. Whenever our family needs a relaxing change-of-pace we play Rook, a low-key, non-pressuring game. A playful game.

Do you know that as recently as the nineteenth century the following church school policy statement was enforced: "We prohibit play in the strongest terms; for those who play when they are young will play when they are old."

On the contrary, authentic religion encourages, nay, requires play. Our days are sadder and emptier when void of playfulness.

**October
7**

THROUGH DOING

"People become house builders through building houses, harp players through playing the harp. We grow to be just by doing things which are just."

Aristotle

This maxim is easy to understand yet difficult to accomplish. It is tempting to get caught up in the quicksand of nice feelings and appealing attitudes.

I have learned that I *behave* rather than *believe* myself into most significant changes.

October
8 SHUV

The Old Testament view of forgiveness is contained in a verb that dominates its penitential literature, the Hebrew word *shuv*, meaning to turn, to return.

The doctrine implies that we have the power to turn from evil to good, and the very act of turning will bring God's forgiveness.

In the new Testament, repent means to change directions, to turn totally around.

Our egos are so huge and defensive sometimes that we are loathe to confess our wrongdoing, to turn about, to switch paths. Yet that very turning around, whether with a child or partner, employee or neighbor is the mark of the large human being.

The seasons turn, and so should we.

CICERO AND DEMOSTHENES

Reaching back to Cicero and Demosthenes, when comparing himself to John F. Kennedy, Adlai Stevenson noted ruefully, "When Cicero had finished speaking, the people said: 'How well he spoke, but when Demosthenes had finished speaking, the people said, 'Let's march!'"

I reflect upon this story after my own speeches. Often, I'm afraid, I stir hearts without moving bodies.

The final measure of one's presentation to an audience is how many attitudes were altered and how many behaviors changed.

THROUGH TOUCHING

"The only way we can overcome our loneliness is through Touching."

Hyemeyohsts Storm

The Native Americans are so committed to Touching that they capitalize it.

The emphasis here is not on being touched, important as that is, but on touching people, earth, things. Touch brings us health and reduces loneliness because we make connection.

My wife and I have always felt that if we want to do something worthwhile for our children, we should create an environment where thay can touch as much as often as possible.

It starts with our own Touching.

**October
11   THE FIRST LADY**

"No one can make you feel inferior without your consent."

Eleanor Roosevelt

This is the birthday (1884) of Eleanor Roosevelt. In countless polls, both national and international, she has been selected as "one of the world's most admired women."

The only woman in American history to serve as the First Lady of our land for a dozen years, Roosevelt was a brilliant and compassionate leader.

At her death, one of her friends phrased it poignantly, "Eleanor would rather light candles than curse the darkness, and her glow has warmed the world."

Or, in her own words, "When you cease to make a contribution you begin to die."

LIKE COLUMBUS...

"The known is finite, the unknown infinite; intellectually we stand on an islet in the midst of an illimitable ocean...Our business in every generation is to reclaim a little more land."

T. H. Huxley

The first Europeans to land in the Americas were adventurers from Norway, Iceland, or Greenland in the late tenth and early eleventh centuries. They certainly settled briefly in New Foundland and may have landed elsewhere on the Atlantic coast of North America.

Nonetheless, Columbus's expedition was distinguished for being the first recorded European expedition to cross the Atlantic Ocean in warm or temperate latitudes. It entailed much longer ocean passages than previously undertaken.

Like Columbus, we don't all make initial discoveries. Most of us will uncover little, if anything, very original during our lifetimes. Our gifts resemble those of Columbus. We bring something special to what already exists.

We make the same voyages as our predecessors but in our own inimitable ways.

October 13

ALL MY BAGS ARE PACKED

"I was reminded of what the late Pope John XXIII said when he was dying. He was asked if everything was as satisfactory as it could be considering the circumstances. He smiled and said: 'All my bags are packed.'"

Ira Sandperl

People whose lives are fulfilled have their spiritual houses in order. They have separated the wheat from the chaff.

They pursue possibilities within their limits.

They neither overrate nor undergrade their gifts.

They serve others.

They do not postpone living.

They are prepared for their date with death.

October 14

DO PEOPLE WEIGH YOU DOWN?

"Do people weigh you down? Don't carry them on your shoulders. Take them into your heart."

Dom Helder Camara

Camara, twice a nominee for the Nobel Peace Prize, has been Archbishop of Olinda in Brazil, the poorest and least developed part of the country.

People often weigh us down because we treat them as burdens rather than as companions. They represent nothing more to us than economic problems, family loads, social misfits, or emotional laggards.

People can be difficult, but they need not be considered onerous.

We are lighter when taken to each other's bosoms.

GIVE AND TAKE

*"The motto of life is 'give and take'.
Everyone must be both a giver and a
receiver. They who are not both are as
barren trees."*

Hasidic saying

Some people say that it is more
blessed to give than to receive. Others
say it is more blessed to receive than to
give.

What is truly blessed, I believe, is
when we give, to give eagerly and
generously, and when we receive, to
receive gratefully and joyously.

When we pay close attention to our
daily endeavors, giving-and-receiving are
often intertwined. In our giving we
receive, and in our receiving we render a
gift.

WE ARE ENLIGHTENERS

"You are the light of the *world*. A *city* set on a hill cannot be hid. Nor do people light a lamp and put it under a bushel, but on a stand, and it gives light to all in the *house*. Let your light so shine before others, that they may see your good works and give glory to your Father who is in heaven."

Matthew 5:14-16

We are lights and lamps, and the only way we can do our job is to shine forth where there is darkness, to give warmth where there is cold, to lead fiery lives ablaze with justice and compassion.

Where are we to burn brightly? Certainly not under a bushel. There are three main areas. In the world or larger sphere, in the city or our local community, and in the house or our own residence.

Some people are great lights in one of the three but sources of darkness in the others.

Our mission is to balance our witness as lights, to enlighten world, city, and home.

FAIL FORWARD

*"Another ball game lost! Good grief! I get
tired of losing...everything I do, I lose!"*
    *"Look at it this way, Charlie Brown,"
says Lucy, "We can learn more from
losing than we do from winning!"*
*"Hey, that makes me the smartest person
in the world!"*

Charles Schulz

Poor Charlie Brown could use more successes under his belt in order to transform his defeatist attitude.

Conversely, most of us need permission to lose, the right to be wrong, the green light not to be perfect. We need freedom to fail even when it really hurts, where much is at stake, in "performance" areas such as academics, sexuality, work, and parenting. We need to lose without giving ourselves the label "loser."

If we love ourselves, then mistakes won't damage our identity. We will maximize the lessons learned from our blunders. Our losses become instructive rather than destructive.

It is called the art of failing forward.

UNTIL I ARRIVE

*"My interest is in the future because I'm
going to spend the rest of my life there."*

Chris Kettering

Abe Lincoln was riding the
Sangamon, Illinois County Court circuit
one severe winter with two of his friends.

His companions were worrying
about the hazards of crossing the
swollen, turbulent, icy Fox River. They
asked him, "Abe, what are we going to
do when we reach the Fox River ford?"

He answered, "I never cross the Fox
River ford until I get to it."

There are different ways of
addressing our tomorrows. My approach
is to think my future through before I
face it. I fantasize about the dangers and
possibilities of what lies ahead. It relaxes
and prepares me for the actuality.

Others, like Lincoln, put tomorrows
out of mind. Thinking about them is
unnerving.

You and I do what works best for
each of us.

TAKING IN AND POURING OUT

"What we take in by contemplation, we must pour out in love."

Meister Eckhart

We are reminded that those who hunger and thirst for justice are blessed (Matthew 5:6), not necessarily those who hunger and thirst for spiritual growth.

It is possible to be preoccupied with our own development and bypass our neighbor, thereby missing our human destiny. Healthy privacy dares not slip into privatism.

We need to balance the inward search with outward fruits.

WISDOM IS RARE ENOUGH

Justice Frankfurter was once asked why he changed his opinion in two widely separate Supreme Court cases on the same subject. He replied, "Wisdom too often never comes, so one ought not to reject it because it comes late."

Here was an open person willing to change his mind when fresh evidence arrived. New insights terrify rigid persons. Flexible individuals, like Frankfurter, receive them with open hearts and arms.

What a delight to be in the presence of a wise, growing person.

THE CHARITY OF ANGER

"One of our greatest obligations is anger."

Nikos Kazantzakis

Anger need not be hostile. We all feel angry and need to wrestle with those near us, especially loved ones.

Anger can be a charitable emotion if we share it wisely. When we fight, and fight we will, let us do so for impact not injury, to deepen communication not construct walls.

Wisdom recommends that we neither flee from nor camouflage our anger but express it without attacking.

Anger is not the opposite of love; indifference is.

CARVED CHERRY STONES

George Moore wrote of Guy de Maupassant's stories that they were merely "carved cherry stones."

Too many of us produce slews of "carved cherry stones" in our work. The products are clever, cute, and attractive but worthless, except for collectors.

It is interesting, but insufficient, to apply our skills to miniature themes. We need to tackle larger issues. Painting pebbles to be used as paperweights, or producing carved cherry stones, is a hobby not a vocation.

We will be measured by the size and scope of our concerns, hopes, loves.

NEVERTHELESS

*"When Henrik Ibsen, the Norwegian
dramatist, came to die, his last word was
'Nevertheless'. As a critic of society, it was
fitting that this should be his last word."*

Halford Luccock

Her life had been a series of
frustrations and traumas, nevertheless
she was glad to be alive.

We unitedly mount an effort,
nevertheless remain sensitive to the
caution of those who disagree with us.

He was sure he made the right
decision to leave a position, nevertheless
he lives well with his choice.

I quarrel with my country,
nevertheless love her.

TRUE PATRIOTISM

"Our feet should be planted in our country, but our eyes should survey the world."

George Santayana

This is the posture of the true patriot. On the contrary, the sights of the chauvinist never extend beyond his or her own precious turf.

We hunger for a global mentality in our contemporary world. We need individuals who prize stories of their own nation while serving the ideals of international life.

Such is the vision of the United Nations.

October
25   **FRIENDS**

*"It was a marvelous period in the womb,
and I shall never forget it. I had almost
everything one could ask for—except
friends. And a life without friends is no life,
however snug and secure it may be."*

Henry Miller

Some of us choose to hide out in the
womb, remaining as secure and snug as
possible. Solitariness is desirable, but it
extracts a heavy price.

Human beings are built for social
intimacy, for friendship. Henry Miller
writes on:

*"A friend must be someone as close
to you as your skin, someone who
imparts color, drama, meaning to
your life."*

LIVELY MINDS

*Anyone who has begun to think places
some portion of the world in jeopardy."*

John Dewey

Mark Twain once counseled a
neighbor: "Take your mind out and
dance on it; it's getting all caked up."

Periodically I take my mind on wild
roller coaster rides. It gets stodgy and
"caked up" dealing with comfortable,
familiar notions.

My mind gets lazy. It hardens. It
needs to be taken out for a fresh whirl
around the dance floor.

If my nerve fails, I hope one of my
buddies will ask it for a dance.

NO SYNONYM

*"No synonym for God is so perfect as
beauty. Whether as seen carving the lines
of the mountains with glaciers, or gathering matter into stars, or planning the
movements of water, or gardening—still
all is beauty."*

John Muir

Muir's whole life is tribute to the
grandeur of beauty. He equated God
with the highest and best he knew.

Others would claim that God is best
captured by goodness. Servants of
compassion and seekers of truth create a
case for their virtues approximating God.

God has a polymorphous nature
which embraces yet transcends the
highest human experiences and values
we know.

There is no single synonym for God.

AGAIN AND THEN AGAIN

*"What makes people of genius, or rather,
what they make, is not new ideas; it is the
ideas by which they are obsessed that
what has been said still has not been said
enough."*

Eugene Delacroix

In our fetish to say something
original or do something unique we forget
that pivotal truths need repetition.

We need to learn and repeat
fundamentals day in and day out.

One of my fundamentals is this:
nothing matters unless performed with
faithfulness to love. If our children master
this fundamental, or at least wrestle with
it mightily, then they are ready to
graduate from our household.

October 29

AND I THINK

*"And I **think** that I have the spirit of God."*

I Corinthians 7:40

In matters of importance it is crucial to hold a humble posture such as Paul did in his letter to the church at Corinth.

Religion and politics comprise too many individuals who are unwilling to be unsure. They definitely know or are absolutely convinced, thus closing doors to further evidence.

Every true believer should heed Oliver Cromwell's sound words: "Believe by the bowels of Christ that ye may be mistaken."

RECOVERING

*"The world breaks everyone; then some
become strong at the broken places."*

Ernest Hemingway

The fellowship of sufferers is the
largest clan in existence. Some have paid
more dues than others, but all share
membership in the club.

We are broken people. Our relationships break as well as our bones. What
matters is whether we become weak or
strong at the broken places. Do we mend
or stay in disrepair?

We never fully recover from ail-
ments, troubles, losses. We are merely in
different stages of recovery. Alcoholics
Anonymous reminds its members that no
one is a *recovered* but always a
recovering alcoholic.

A sobering thought.

BLUNDERING SAINTS

"The wonderful thing about saints is that they are human. They lose their tempers, get hungry, scold God, are egotistical or testy or impatient in their turns, make mistakes and regret them. Still they go on doggedly, blundering toward heaven."

Phyllis McGinley

Today is Halloween, all-saints eve. It is time to reflect upon the saints, the strugglers, the searchers. Persons like Jacob who have been wrestling all night long only to emerge lame but triumphant at dawn.

Think about individuals you have known directly or indirectly whose word or deed has enlarged your horizon, given you courage to take a stand, carry on.

Give thanks for them in the silence of your heart.

NOVEMBER

A WAY

"We will either find a way or make one."

Hannibal

Sometimes a way to do something is given to us. We don't think about it; another presents it to us, out of the blue.

Other times, if we are alert, we are likely to find a way toward solving our problem or addressing our concern.

Occasionally, we look and look, and no opening is available. Brush impedes our path. Then we have no alternative but to cut a route through to the other side. We make our future.

Finally, although Hannibal didn't admit it, there are occasions when we can't go forward and our best plan is to pause and ponder while standing still.

CREATIVE INSECURITY

*"Probably the only place where someone
can feel really secure is in a maximum
security prison, except for the imminent
threat of release."*

Germane Greer

No corner of absolute security exists
on earth. We are destined to live amid
creative insecurity, from morning until
night.

We can lose a job. Relationships end
in sadness. Ethical decisions are riddled
with ambiguities. Even the scientific
world baffles.

The fact that nothing can be
fastened down makes life more
interesting. It keeps our minds alive and
our spirits on edge.

WORKING THE SUM OUT

*"Many people reach their conclusions
about life like lazy school children. They
copy the answers from the back of the
book without troubling to work out the
sum for themselves."*

Soren Kierkegaard

Woody Allen states that his friend
cheated on the metaphysical exam of life
when she gazed into the soul of her
neighbor.

We take counsel from our peers.
Those who fail to take advice, when
appropriate, are arrogant. Nevertheless,
each of us is accountable for authoring
lives truthful to ourselves and loving of
others.

Each of us must "work out the sum
for ourselves."

November
4   A LITTLE MORE

"When through one person a little more love and goodness, a little more light and truth come into the world, then that person's life has had meaning."

We shy away from making contributions to society, because we believe the results will be modest.

In truth, few of us change the world substantially. But each of us can make a difference. We possess unique gifts, however limited.

Instead of trying to move mountains, we can start by shoveling dirt in the foothills. Instead of waiting to deliver one great deed, we can perform several decent acts along the way.

A little bit of goodness and love go a long, long way toward beautifying our universe.

MANY PATHWAYS

"God chooses one person with a shout, another with a song, another with a whisper."

Rabbi Nahman of Bratislav

Gurus are dime a dozen, especially spiritual ones. Someone, somewhere will hand you a pamphlet on ultimate truth that may seduce you into their camp.

Universal religion proclaims that there isn't simply one pathway to fulfillment or serenity but many. Through trial and error we find a spiritual discipline fitting our temperament and desires.

God chooses us through various means, and we do likewise with God.

SING OUT!

"The woods would be very silent if only those birds sang out who sing the best."

Anonymous

We refuse to participate in some activity because we don't feel confident of our capability. An inferiority complex keeps us from risking participation.

Yet the woods hanker for the sounds of all its birds. So do our lives. We might be surprised by some of the exquisite, intriguing sounds waiting to be released in our souls.

PEACE—EARTH

"It is in each of us that the peace of the world is cast...in the frontiers of our hearts, from there it must spread out to the limits of the universe."

Cardinal Suenens

In Russian, the word for peace is exactly the same as the word for earth. When the Soviets say "Peace on Earth," the terms are interchangeable.

Our understanding of peace must be as expansive as the size of the globe. A peace that is pursued within the confines of our own hearts is too small. A peace that extends to our family and friends, but no farther, is not large enough.

We are placed on earth to bring peace to the entire planet. We are restless until our job is completed.

November 8   THIS IS THE DAY

"This is the day the Lord hath made; we will rejoice and be glad in it."

Psalm 118

We didn't have anything to do with creation. We don't have anything to do with ensuing mornings either. We can't make days like God, but we can enjoy them. That's our calling.

Come what may, tragedy or happiness, we are to treat each day with joy. Before we scrutinize or slice it up, we are to "be glad in it."

PARTING FROM PREJUDICES

"It is never too late to give up our prejudices."

Henry David Thoreau

We play favorites from the moment we emerge from the womb. As babies we establish primary connections with those nearest and dearest in our empire. We are wary of outsiders. We are uneasy with strange things.

As we grow up, the challenge is to avoid the hardened attitude of estrangement. Differences are to be tolerated, even appreciated. When they are sources of arrogance or alienation, prejudices are born.

Some prejudices are modest, others more pronounced, even pernicious. In every case, we can eradicate the bulk of them.

Say farewell to one prejudice today.

TALKIN' AND LISTENIN'

"Great Uncle George, who was in his 80's, wandered across the street to chat with a neighbor until dinner time. Considerably overdue when he returned, Uncle George explained without apology: 'I got to talkin' with Mr. Sherwood, and he just couldn't seem to stop listenin'.'"

Gordon Loos

For every vigorous talker, there needs to be an active listener. Both parties are essential to strike up communication. If one side quits, dialogue is broken.

The variations are subtle. A talker has the responsibility to be thoughtful, neither heavy nor egocentric. Hearers need to be patient and assertive rather than callous or submissive.

Taking turns is imperative too.

SMILINGLY UNRAVELED

*"There is no cutting of the Gordian knots
of life. Each must be smilingly unraveled."*

Robert Louis Stevenson

The Gordian knot was tied by
Gordius, King of Phrygia, purported to
be capable of being untied only by the
future ruler of Asia, and cut by
Alexander the Great with his sword.

We know the Gordian knot as an
intricate problem, especially a problem
insoluble in its own terms.

Over the long haul, whether in
politics, partnerships, or parenting, we
fare better through persuasion than
coercion. Certain decisions can't be
forced. Manipulation works with
immature people; strong folks won't be
maneuvered.

I don't know of any person or
problem that isn't better served by being
smilingly unraveled.

MOVING RIGHT ALONG

"I find the great thing in this world is not so much where we stand, as in what direction we are moving."

Oliver Wendell Holmes

Everyone stands somewhere. The important matter is where our feet are pointed. Even being pigeon-toed, it is clear that my feet point in a basic direction wherever I plant myself. The direction where they point is the direction in which I will be moving next.

Choose where you stand. Stand firmly not idly. Then start walking ahead. It's not very complicated, is it?

WATCHING AND LOVING

"When I touch that flower, I am touching infinity. I learn what I know by watching and loving everything."

George Washington Carver

Today we pay homage to George Washington Carver (1864-1943), the outstanding black U.S. chemurgist and experimenter, who devoted his life to agricultural research for the betterment of the South and his people.

Carver was born of slave parentage in Missouri. Eager for education, he worked his way through school and onward to greatness.

Did you know that from the peanut alone Carver made some 300 products, including cheese, coffee, ink, and soap? In 1940 he donated his savings of $33,000 to establish the Carver Foundation to carry on his research.

I like the blend in his statement. "I learn what I know by watching and loving everything." Keen observation and profound compassion are hallmarks of the capable scientist, of any capable person.

SELF-DISCLOSURE

"The Delphic Oracle advised, 'Know Thyself'; I would say, 'Make Thyself known and then Thou wilt know Thyself.'"

Sidney Jourard

We are more likely to know our beings as we dare to reveal them. Total self-disclosure is neither possible nor desirable, but too many of us are walking, expurgated versions.

We monitor and censor behavior and revelations in order to create an image of ourselves that we want others to have.

No one is helped in phony, partial portrayals. Our neighbor is fooled; we are fraudulent. Both parties suffer.

November
15   **REDS OR GREENS?**

Two apples up in a tree were looking down on the world. The first apple said, "Look at all those people fighting, robbing, rioting—no one seems willing to get along with anyone else. Someday we apples will be the only ones left. Then we'll rule the world."

Replied the second apple, "Which of us—the reds or the greens?"

We are so quick to condemn the lifestyle in another land and rapid to praise our own. Soviets and Americans are especially skilled at such arrogance.

Frequently in the history of the world, groups have revolted for valid reasons, only to abandon those reasons once in power. In the Old Testament, it reads: "Justice, justice shalt thou follow!" (Deuteronomy 16:20). Why is the word justice repeated? Because we must always follow justice with justice, not with unrighteousness; love with love, not with hate.

BEYOND REASON

"We die on the day when our lives cease to be illumined by the steady radiance renewed daily of a wonder the source of which is beyond reason."

Dag Hammarskjöld

Reason is an approach, a tool to facilitate growing, but there are times when we leap in faith beyond reason to embrace a person, cause, or conviction.

The wonder Hammarskjöld refers to might be the wonder of unimagined love, unspeakable strength, unmerited forgiveness, and the source of all such wonders carries us beyond reason.

Reason can't get its logical arms around wonder.

Today is Carolyn's and my wedding anniversary. Our marriage travels beyond reason. It dwells in wonder.

November 17   WOBBLING WASTES ENERGY

"If you sit, just sit. If you walk, just walk. But whatever you do, don't wobble."

Zen

We not only confuse others with our behavior; we confound our own emotional systems. We want to walk, but we end up sitting down. This incongruence results in "driving the car with the brakes on."

Once we decide to master the word processor, let's go ahead and do it. Instead of dreaming about playing the flute, let's finger it. In commitment, we dash the hopes of a thousand potential selves.

We would do well to quit focusing on our *potential* selves and spend more time being our *actual* selves.

Whether we choose to sit or walk, let us do it exuberantly. Wobbling wastes energy and motion.

THE GREATEST OF THESE?

*"Paul wrote that of faith, hope, and love,
love was the greatest of these. But I do not
think that is so. If we have no faith, but
only have love, what could we possibly do
with that love?"*

Brandoch Lovely

Love by itself can be a powerless
virtue. It is activated by the nudging and
nurture of other values.

Love without courage seldom leaves
home.

Love without hope risks little.

Love without justice can be
undiscerning.

Love without anger becomes
sentimentalized.

Love without humor is ponderous.

THE HINDERER

"The name Satan means in Hebrew the hinderer. That is the correct designation for the anti-human individuals in the human race. Let us not allow this satanic element in us to hinder us from realizing ourselves...let us dare, despite all, to trust!"

Martin Buber

To hinder means to cause harmful or annoying delay or interference with progress. Whatever hinders us from the pursuit of authentic humanity is a kind of Satan.

One of the challenges of progressive spiritual life is to eliminate, as methodically as possible, those habits in our lives which impede us from openness, which obstruct us from loving, which block us from experiencing the joys and beauties of existence.

**November
20**

KEEP ON IN
YOUR STRUGGLE

*"I like human beings. I'm glad I'm one of
them. But I think we're irrational. Look at
our race prejudice, look at our inability to
get out of war, look at the crazy things we
do in our personal lives. My optimism is
diminishing and yet the law of my life is that
it's worthwhile to keep on in our struggle."*

Norman Thomas

Norman Thomas weighed only four
pounds when born on November 20, 1884.
The last idealist, as he was affectionately
called by many, survived his tenuous
beginnings and grew to prodigious
strength of personality and character.

It might be said that Norman Thomas
failed. He ran again and again for public
office, six times as a candidate for the
Presidency, but his only victory was
election to the New York school board.

Throughout his life he felt it was
"worthwhile to keep on in our struggle"
for peace and justice. His life was
governed by unflinching principles of the
right and good that he not only preached
but practiced.

I don't call that failure.

THREE KINDS OF PEOPLE

"Speak to the children of Israel that they go forward."
Exodus 14:15

John Haynes Holmes once commented on three kinds of people among the Israelites in their march through the desert.

One group wanted to go back to Egypt. They preferred slavery to the uncertainty of the wilderness.

The second group was satisfied wherever they might be at night. They were content to gather the manna as it came.

The third group, the smallest, wanted to go forward. Moses was among their number. He heard God say to him, "Speak to the children of Israel that they go forward."

In our own tongue, these are respectively the spiritual, moral, and social reactionaries, conservatives, and progressives. They are the people of yesterday, today, and tomorrow.

I find myself in all three states. Sometimes I even feel them battling one another for ascendancy in my being.

I struggle to go forward.

November
22 **SECRET SORROWS**

"Believe me, we all have our secret sorrows, which the world knows not; and oftentimes we call people cold when they are only sad."

Henry Wadsworth Longfellow

We carry in our bosoms singular, piercing hurts. Even unmentionable ones. They may seldom, if ever, see the light of day yet remain real.

We harbor unspeakable joys too—experiences too marvelous to convey. But it is the inexpressible sorrows that seem most poignant. Our stolid exteriors camouflage wounded interiors.

We accept one another more readily when we acknowledge our secret sorrows.

A HOBGOBLIN

"Consistency is the hobgoblin of little minds."

Ralph Waldo Emerson

I heard of the judge who asked a man his age. He replied, "Thirty!" The judge said, "You've given that age in the court for the last five years." The man replied, "Yes, I know, but I'm not one of those who say one thing today and another thing tomorrow."

There is some virtue in consistency, but, on the whole, it is over-rated.

First, consistency is only valuable if we are consistent in doing the right things.

Second, there is merit to what Oscar Wilde said, "Consistency is the last refuge of the unimaginative." We need to leap out of ruts, savor life, vary our agendas. Instead of rising at 6:05, try getting up at 5:06!

Third, inconsistency is often necessitated by changes which are based on moral growth. Gandhi was asked why he could so easily contradict this week what he had said just last week.

He replied that it was because this week he knew better.

DON'T TAKE DUMB RISKS!

"Religion is not taking dumb risks with things you value highly."

Larry McGinty

We all take risks.

The sensitive, vital person can't help but take them daily. The trick is not to take "dumb" risks but bright, reasonable ones.

There is a fine but clear line between being adventurous and foolish.

It is especially important not to make stupid moves with our professional life, our social conscience, our loved ones.

A THRASHING

"Nothing is so healthy as a thrashing at the proper time, and from very few won games have I learned as much as I have from most of my defeats."

Jose Capablanca

Capablanca wasn't merely a good loser who never tasted the fruits of victory. Nearly a half-century ago, he was the greatest chess player in the world. When he speaks of loss, one listens.

I recently received various thrashings: a rejection notice concerning a professional project, an injury which resisted healing, unexpected tennis losses, and deaths of friends.

Our lives sometimes deepen more from losses than triumphs.

WOUNDS OF A FRIEND

"Faithful are the wounds of a friend."

Proverbs 27:6

Friends salute our virtues and call us on our faults, and through it all, accept us for who we truly are.

Everyone of us has fairweather pals who wouldn't dream of going tiger-hunting with us when asked to do so. There are also those so-called buddies who have a need to parent or soothe us, showing up when we're needy. They just can't wait to try out their latest messianic ploy on us.

Those two types are half-friends. Sometimes they are just who we want. Most of the time we hanker after full-fledged friends. We desire a handful of individuals in our life who are ambidextrous, comforting and confronting with agility.

The Old Testament reminds us that "faithful are the wounds of a friend!"

Let us give special thanks for the faithful wounders in our lives. They are rare indeed.

NOTICING

"It is noticing things that puts them in the room, it is ignoring them that takes them out."

Marcel Proust

Things, people, realities move between foreground and background in our lives.

At times, a certain thought is center stage. Then it recedes. Another notion thrusts itself into prominence. We ignore something else for the time being.

Our noticing wields power. It brings the outside into focus, that which is external inside.

Proust urges us to ponder this: if you want something to be central to your life, then notice it with an eye born of respect and caring.

Notice it with a lifeful of gratitude this Thanksgiving season.

HE RUINED MY LIFE

One day Ira Sandperl walked past a bookstore and saw, in the window, a picture of a skinny brown man in a loincloth, sitting at a spinning wheel.

Ira had no money with him at the time, but said he would come back and pay for the book the next day, if the clerk would let him take it home. The clerk said that anyone interested in that book was not likely to be dishonest, and he gave Ira the book.

"Gandhi, the rat!" says Ira. "He ruined my life!" Ira fell in love with non-violence and gave his life to that philosophy.

So it goes. We meet someone or read something that radically shifts our being, setting us irretrievably on a new path. This collision ruins our life, because it makes us face up to realities we would rather ignore.

A LITTLE WORLD

"A little world I possess, where thought and feelings dwell; and very hard the task I find of governing it well."

Louisa May Alcott

Louisa May Alcott, writer, was born in Germantown, Pennsylvania on November 29, 1832. Her father was Bronson Alcott, transcendentalist and educator. Her mother was Abigail May, advocate of abolition.

In addition to writing, Alcott was active in reform movements of temperance and suffrage. She had little patience with idle philosophizing and remarked: "Why discuss the 'unknowable' until our poor are fed and the wicked saved."

Her goal in life was to beautify her "little world" within the larger universe.

CRUEL BUT KIND

"I am cruel to ideas, but kind to people."

Martin Buber

We can be intolerant of what people do while maintaining a level of acceptance for the doers. I used to think "cruel" was too strong a term here. Not anymore.

Sometimes we don't like something, but we modify the sharpness of our objection when we ought to be tougher. To be cruel is to be fierce, abrasive, rough.

Many situations require a cruel yet humane response.

DECEMBER

December 1 — LIGHTS THAT KEEP SHINING

"The light shines in the darkness, and the darkness has not overcome it."

John 1:5

We live by lights that keep shining.

There is the light of unmerited love and spontaneous laughter.

There is the light of a long-awaited insight breaking into our listless lives.

There is the light of someone thanking us when our spirits feel bedraggled.

There is the light of illumination when our minds are dried up.

The darkness comes. Nonetheless, it cannot overpower those moments of light shining. They are invincible. They provide warmth and fire for our journey.

December
2   L'ARN

Charles Beard long ago remarked how sorry he was that the word *l'arn*, seasoned by hard service in New England, should have gone completely out of currency as a transitive verb.

"You can't teach a person anything," he said, "and certainly you can't learn them anything, but maybe you can l'arn them something."

We nourish the fragile self-concept of our children, pushing and caressing in compassionate rhythm. We instruct and inspire. We share our own gaps and awarenesses.

We parents never cease being in the business of l'arning our loved ones and being l'arned by them in return.

December
3   HERE COMES TRUTH!

"Truth comes in small installments."

People hanker to "find the whole truth, and nothing but the truth, so help me God"—preferably all at once. Conversely, I agree with Oliver Wendell Holmes, Jr. who remarked: "I don't believe or know anything about absolute truth."

We obtain pieces of wisdom here and there. Some scientific truth now and some political savvy later, some moral insight in the morning and a religious revelation nestled in the corner of an evening.

"Truth comes in small installments" to my neck of the woods. It's enough. I neither expect nor need more than I receive.

BEYOND WORDS

"If I could tell you in words what I meant, I wouldn't have needed to dance it."

Isadora Duncan

Backstage, dancer Isadora Duncan was asked what she was trying to convey by a dance she had performed. Her answer is our quote for the day.

Frequently, we are unable to express our feelings or convictions in words. We need another medium. It is important to vary the ways in which we communicate: through dance, pictures, touch. The ways of expression are manifold.

As a young child I was unusually quiet. Up to four or so I seldom spoke. Maybe I had nothing important to say. Perhaps I couldn't find the words to convey my soul.

When I began to speak I took off and have been reasonably verbal ever since. But the long periods of silence in my early life helped me appreciate the value of non-verbal sharing.

Explore the myriad ways of revealing your karma.

DRIVE AWAY DISTRACTIONS

"If at prayer we do nothing but drive away temptations and distractions, our prayer is well made."

St. Francis de Sales

We expect too much from prayer. Whether we meditate a few minutes per day or contemplate for hours, we anticipate earth-shaking results.

We would be wiser to appreciate modest returns. Any release from tension during our frantic lives is welcome.

It doesn't take much to grant sufficient serenity to face our grueling moments.

WE ARE RENEWABLE

"All that matters is that one is created anew."

Galatians 6:15

Our first birth doesn't really count for much. The later births shape and refine our personhood. We need to be "created anew" daily.

We need to remind ourselves, especially when we are down, that we are renewable. No matter what we do, we can take advantage of fresh chances. We can turn around. We are forgiven. We can start again.

Sometimes we are created anew by intentional efforts. Other times it is a gift beyond our doing.

Rejoice in your renewability.

**December
7**   **YET MORE LOVING**

*"Awake at dawn with a winged heart, and
give thanks for another day of loving."*

Kahlil Gibran

This is a fragment from one of
Gibran's prose-poems. It serves as the
daily greeting of those who share
moments of reflection upon rising.

Many of us are able to offer
gratitude at the close of the day,
particularly if it has been a fortunate one.
Few are those who, upon climbing out of
bed in the morning, are spirited enough
to say thanks not for a result but for an
opportunity: the chance to respond to life
with yet more loving.

A LITTLE KINDER

"It's a bit embarrassing to have been concerned with the human problem all one's life and find at the end that one has no more to offer than: 'Try to be a little kinder!'"

Aldous Huxley

Wise and conscientious laborers in the vineyards often come to the close of their lives realizing that clear, simple truths prevail.

The purpose of life is nothing particularly fancy or complicated. It comes down to being kind, kinder, kindest.

Hopefully, we learn this wisdom early on in our lives.

A CLOISTERED VIRTUE

"I have contempt for a fugitive and cloistered virtue, unexercised and unbreathed, that never sallies out and sees her adversary, but slinks out of the race where that immortal garland is to be run for, not without dust and heat."

John Milton

This great English poet, statesperson, essayist, and proponent of free thought was born today in 1608.

His quote reminds me of the line in Pasternak's novel, *Dr. Zhivago,* "I don't like people who have never fallen or stumbled. Their virtue is lifeless and of little value. Life has not revealed its beauty to them."

Pure and unsullied virtues are worthless. Honesty kept to oneself, love unexpressed, courage voiced only in one's closet, justice in the abstract are not true virtues but floating ideals.

Only when risked in the frays of life, however, imperfectly, do virtues emerge as virtues.

NEWS AND POEMS

*"It is difficult to get the news from poems
yet we die miserably every day for lack of
what is found there."*

William Carlos Williams

Some people live on a diet of
information with smatterings of
inspiration. Malnutrition results.

Our spiritual system needs both
news and poetry, data and uplift. Our
lives hunger for balance. For every news
program, our hearts yearn for some
music. For every glance at the business
page, our spirits gravitate to the comic
section. Along with scouring international
events, we need moments of quiet
reflection.

December
11 CRITICS

"If you judge people, you have no time to love them."

Mother Theresa

Most critics are busy scrutinizing and evaluating. They have little energy left for creativity.

We need to be discriminating in our decisions. We must say "yes" to this and "no" to that. We draw lines in our lives. Otherwise, our loving becomes saccharine and fuzzy.

Yet when all is said and done, we live by compassion not criticism.

12   A DEADLINE!

Chaim Potok relates asking father about death when at age six he saw a dead bird: "'Why' I asked. 'That's the way the Ribbono Shel Olom made the world, Asher.' 'Why?' 'So life would be precious, Asher. Something that is yours forever is never precious.'"

Our lives are more sensitive and keen when faced with the prospect of a termination date. We are eager to share full times and loving deeds because we know we won't simply glide on forever.

There are never-before and never-again moments facing you and me today.

December
13   LIFT AND LEAN

"There are two kinds of people on earth: the people who lift and the people who lean."

Ella Wheeler Wilcox

As usual, the spiritual life is not an either/or proposition but a both/and. There is a time to lift and a time to lean. The trick is knowing which to do, when, with whom.

Some of us are prone to do a lot of lifting—lifting this or that cause, this or that person. We are compulsive do-gooders. But servants can suffer themselves right into resentment. Inspirers can wear out if not replenished.

I invite those of us who are inveterate lifters—who serve, support and save ongoingly—to lean, let down, receive bolstering from beyond ourselves.

Then for those times when we need to stop leaning, I encourage us to reach down and lift up an idea, a person, an issue.

348

I SEEM TO BE A VERB

"I live on Earth at present, and I don't know what I am. I know that I am not a category. I am not a thing—a noun. I seem to be a verb, an evolutionary process—an integral function of the universe."

Buckminster Fuller

I depict humans as creatures of verve and vibrancy, action and assertiveness, growing. I tend to romanticize us.

Most earthlings are not verbs at all but nouns, static substances, or adjectives, always modifying but seldom moving forward. Some of us are conjunctions and prepositions, links between entities.

You can't have a sentence without a verb.

Life pales without them, too.

A SEASON TO ITSELF

*"Winter under cultivation is as arable as
Spring."*

Emily Dickinson

Living in the cold country one
discovers two basic life-styles.

There are those who hide from the
elements and those who befriend them.
The former tend to be wandering
despondents for much of the winter, and
the latter are more cheerful because of
engaging in restorative frolic.

The winters outside and inside us
can be arable if cultivated. As my
colleague, Greta Crosby, writes:

> *"Let us not wish away the winter. It
> is a season to itself, not simply the
> way to spring. The clarity and
> brilliance of the winter sky delight. A
> low dark sky can snow, emblem of
> individuality, liberality and aggregate
> power. Let us therefore praise
> winter, rich in beauty, challenge,
> and pregnant negativities."*

PERSPICACITY

"I intend to bring to you strength, joy, courage, perspicacity, defiance."

André Gide

All the qualities Gide promises to deliver are important. I want to focus on the least known of the lot: perspicacity. It is an appropriate gift to receive and offer during the holiday season.

Perspicacity means acute mental vision or discernment. It refers to being savvy and keen. The perspicacious individual literally is one who "sees things through to the heart."

Such people see through the tinsel, the commercialism, the hoopla to the heart of the season: the delivery of generous and genuine love.

The heart of the holidays is to see *beneath* the surface to the underlying spiritual sentiment; *beyond* the literal to the poetic; *behind* the questions of the doubting mind to the answers of the longing heart.

BEING ALONGSIDE

*"One day Joshu fell down and called out,
'Help me up! Help me up!' A monk came
and lay down beside him. Joshu got up
and went away."*

Zen story

The monk didn't try to save Joshu;
he displayed compassion. He literally
"suffered alongside." He joined him. He
"lay down beside him." That act of
support was sufficient.

Joshu then proceeded to lift himself
up, inspired and strengthened by the
monk's companionship.

NO SNOWFLAKE

"No snowflake in an avalanche ever feels responsible."

Stanislaw Lee

The same thing happens when we are cut by a buzz-saw: which tooth in the saw is the culprit? Who knows? When we are bloody and in pain, does it matter?

It is common among us creatures to want praise when, as a member, our group does something noteworthy. Conversely, when society oppresses some of our sisters and brothers, we are apt to point fingers.

When we confess that even the most decent among us exploits others, we are open to making healthy changes.

BURNED TO WHITE ASH

"I want to be thoroughly used up when I die."

George Bernard Shaw

The Zen master Suzuki Roshi said, "One should live their life like a very hot fire, so there is no trace left behind. Everything is burned to white ash."

Zen would have us be utterly mindful to each of our experiences. Each act is to be done fully in the moment. When we are sitting, sit. When we are walking, walk. When we are serving, serve.

Our inability to tune into each moment and be completely present is the bane of our existence. It keeps friends and families light-years apart. It leads to a skewed work commitment.

Living our lives "like a very hot fire" isn't always possible. Our business is sometimes unfinished. There are loose ends in our relationships. We juggle competing attractions upon occasion. Nonetheless, being fully there for self, for others, for the loves of our lives is an aspiration.

As my friend told me, "Tom, live as though every day was your last...and someday you will be right."

PERSONAL

"In an envelope marked: Personal, God addressed me a letter. In an envelope marked: Personal, I have given my answer."

Langston Hughes

Hughes was one of the prominent black writers in the 20th century. He wrote poetry, short stories, autobiography, song lyrics, essays, humor, and plays.

Soren Kierkegaard, the eminent nineteenth century Danish theologian, declared that our lives consisted primarily of receiving letters from God with our home address on it.

Hughes goes one step further: the religious venture is a two-way street between the human and divine. We both have something to say.

God's address and our answers are personal. No one can open up for viewing the correspondence of either.

WINTER SOLSTICE

On December 21, the time of Winter Solstice, we sophisticated moderns and religious faithful believe that the sun will return, that light will conquer darkness, that love will beat out hate in the stables of existence.

We believe it on the evidence. We believe it by faith. We believe it into being. And we live it into being.

While searching amid the darkness for a star, we are also charged to light candles. The transition from darkness to light is a collaboration of the divine and the human, grace and effort.

We are receivers and bringers of light. We illumine and are illumined.

A MULTI-HUED PALETTE

"When I haven't any blue, I use red."

Pablo Picasso

Often we find ourselves thrown into a tizzy of self-pity because we don't have at our disposal a certain color or particular possibility.

When we don't have blue, instead of halting operations, Picasso encourages us to use the other options in our palette: red, green, yellow, lavender, and more.

A monochromatic life is enervating. We need to use with confidence a wide range of the resources in front of us. What we have on hand is more interesting than we imagine.

Ours can be an exquisitely colorful world.

THE MYSTERY OF MISFORTUNE

"Whoever thinks seriously upon the suffering and the injustice of the world will find any false sense of superiority oozing away. In the presence of all the cruelly handicapped, they will say: 'This might be me, yes, and tomorrow it may be me.'"

Arthur Foote

As the saying goes: "There but for the grace of God go you or I," or a friend, or a child, or an associate. Good things happen to bad people and evil things befall lovely people.

It is fruitless to figure out the "why's" of misfortune. We run into roadblocks trying to be rational about the inexplicable mysteries of tragedy.

Humanity is best served by our willingness to face our suffering and grow through, perhaps even beyond, it.

FORGIVE YOUR PARENTS

"Children begin by loving their parents; as they grow older they judge them; sometimes they forgive them."

Oscar Wilde

Loving and judging parents come rather easily to most of us children. Forgiving them is a more difficult process.

Even if our parents are not living, I invite us to devote ourselves to forgiving them for some things they have done that wounded us or stifled our growth. They need our forgiveness; we need to offer it.

After forgiving our parents, we can move on to forgiving our children, friends, foes, finally, our selves.

WORDS BECOME FLESH

"My life, my argument."

Albert Schweitzer

Schweitzer humbly noted: "I am only a person living out my religion."

I too believe in deeds over creeds. As the Gospel of John states: "The Word became flesh. . ." God's love for the world became flesh, literally pitched tent in our midst, was born in Jesus of Nazareth.

That is the primary message on Christmas day.

Our words are wasted until they become flesh, are embodied, pitch tent, are lived out.

Rabbi Moshe of Kobryn said: "When you utter a word before God, then enter into that word with every one of your limbs." One of his listeners asked: "How can a big human being possibly enter into a little word?" "Those who think themselves bigger than the words," said the zaddik "are not the kind of persons we are talking about."

Saying the word "love" is warm-up for "loving."

THE WORK OF CHRISTMAS BEGINS

"When the star in the sky is gone. When the shepherds are back with their flocks— the work of Christmas begins: to find the lost, to heal the broken, to feed the hungry, to release the prisoners, to rebuild the nations, to bring peace among all."

Howard Thurman

We find it easy to be generous and loving during the holidays. We zealously do during December what we have forgotten to do the rest of the year.

Our gentle, compassionate ways must be continued after the celebration ceases and the shepherds are back in the fields. Our Christmas caring prepares us for the tougher calls to mercy and justice that face us once we return to "normal" living.

December
27   PRODUCTIVITY

"Don't tell me how hard you work. Tell me how much you get done."

James Ling

The people I most admire are not activists but resultists. One day they work indefatiguably to achieve desired results. Other days they labor only a while. And they always know when to rest.

They are not interested in setting endurance records. They are pursuing results.

They are producers.

THE ANIMAL THAT LOVES

*"Love creates. Love creates even God, for
how else have we come to God, any of us,
but through love? Human, the scientists
say, is the animal that thinks. They are
wrong. Human is the animal that loves."*

Archibald MacLeish

Love enables our inner and outer
worlds to travel in meaningful circles. I
refer to multiple loves: love of work, love
of God, love of play, love in spite of
doubts and pain, love in midst of joy and
victory.

Love brings us into deeper
communion with selves, neighbors,
nature. Love aspires for a holier world
beyond while enriching the one we
already possess.

It is arrogant to claim that we are
the only animals who love. The beasts of
the field seem to love as well as we do, if
not better. Yet, other species aside, our
human work is clear: love, love, love,
love.

A STING

Henrik Ibsen, the Danish playwright, kept a scorpion by his desk to keep a sting to his words.

I'm not the least bit interested in keeping a scorpion, tarantula, or baby alligator by my bedside. They might do more than bring sting to my words.

I do, however, applaud the sentiment. Whatever it takes to bring both punch and bite to our writings and tasks is valuable. The prod will differ for each of us.

It is tempting to slide through our days. It is tantalizing to say sweet things when the situation cries out for toughness.

We need stinging reminders by our sides.

HITCHED TO EVERYTHING ELSE

"When we try to pick out anything by itself, we find it hitched to everything else in the Universe. The whole wilderness is unity and interrelation is alive and familiar."

John Muir

Perhaps our highest and holiest job is to honor the cosmos as a unified whole.

We don't have to create a uni-verse; we merely have to treat our given one as such.

Being "hitched" ourselves influences every move we make in life.

We praise, give thanks, are filled with awe not in some narcissistic frenzy but in relationship to an other: a human, a god, an event, an animal—realities that transcend yet include us, realities to which we are hitched.

Bob Kegan described us humans as "embedduals." It means that we are individuals who are deeply embedded in the various structures of our wondrous universe.

December
31 HALLELUJAH!

"Somehow I need to know, to sense in every cell, that fringed mystery in which I live. I want to be breathless before the universe. I want exultation and hallelujahs and ecstasy."

Cassi Shea

Amid the hoorays tonight, may there be shouts of hallelujahs too. A hooray is a spontaneous whoopee. A hallelujah is more deliberate. It is measured joy. There should be opportunity for both on New Year's Eve.

A hallelujah is saying not only that I'm glad to be alive but also that I'm grateful to all who brought me into this "fringed mystery in which I live." The mystery of my being is precious and fragile.

Before the balloons go up and we sing "Auld Lang Syne," I invite us to offer some hallelujahs to our family, spiritual ancestors, divine presence, friends, and all our kin in the animal world.

Praise ye—all of ye!

Mail Order Information:

For additional copies of Tom Owen-Towle's books send price per book plus $1.50 for shipping and handling (ADD 6% Sales tax-CA Res.). Make checks payable to Tom Owen-Towle, 3303 Second Avenue, San Diego, California 92103. Telephone (619) 295-7067.

☐ SPIRITUAL FITNESS: DAY BY DAY, $12.00
☐ NEW MEN—DEEPER HUNGERS, $7.95
☐ STAYING TOGETHER, $7.95
☐ GENERATION TO GENERATION, $7.95

Also available through local bookstores that use R.R. Bowker Company BOOKS IN PRINT catalogue system. Order through publisher SUNFLOWER INK for bookstore discount.